AF372079

Tris Vonna-Michell

This publication was supported as Catalogue No. 117 by the Alfried Krupp von Bohlen und Halbach-Stiftung under its support prize "Catalogues for Young Artists".

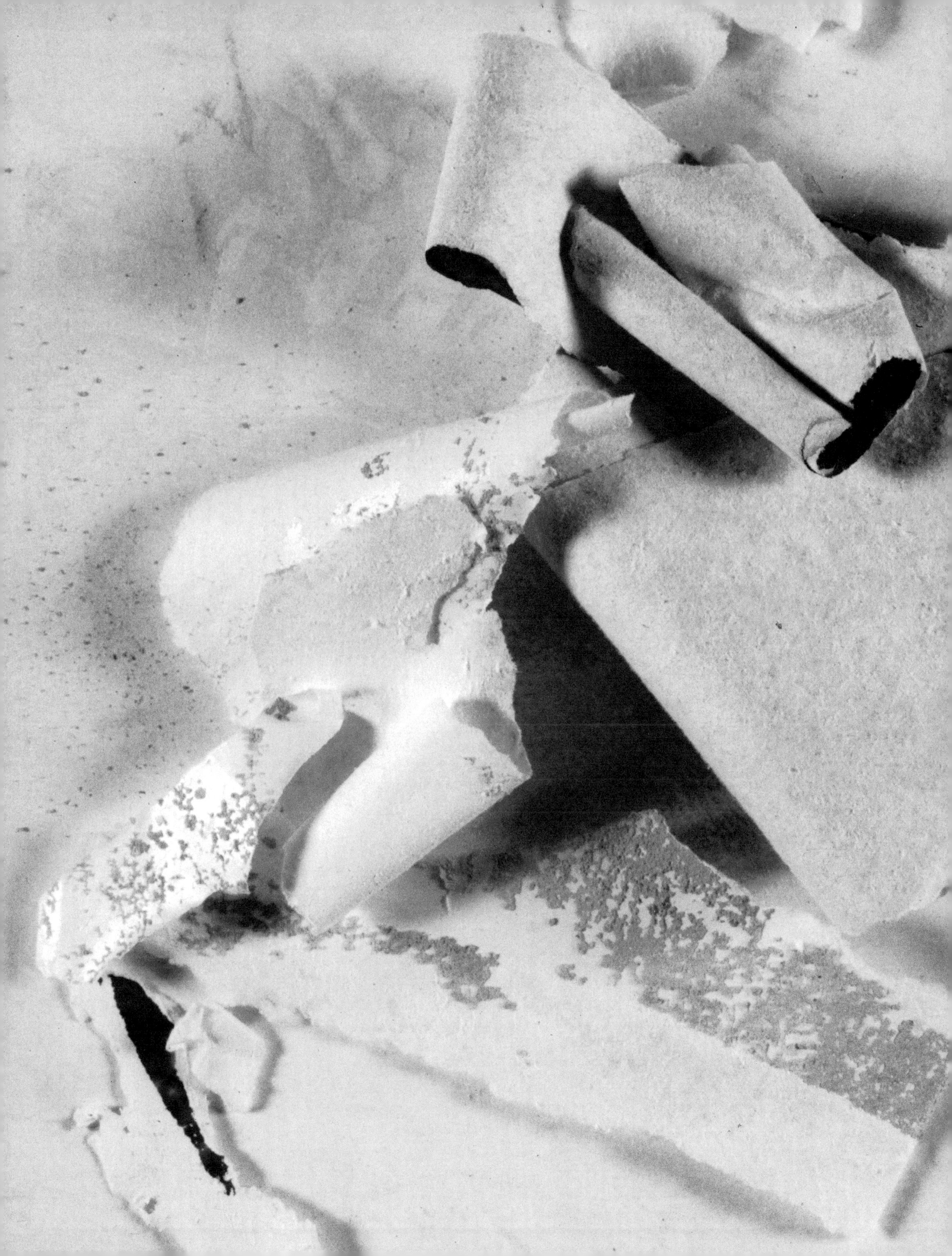

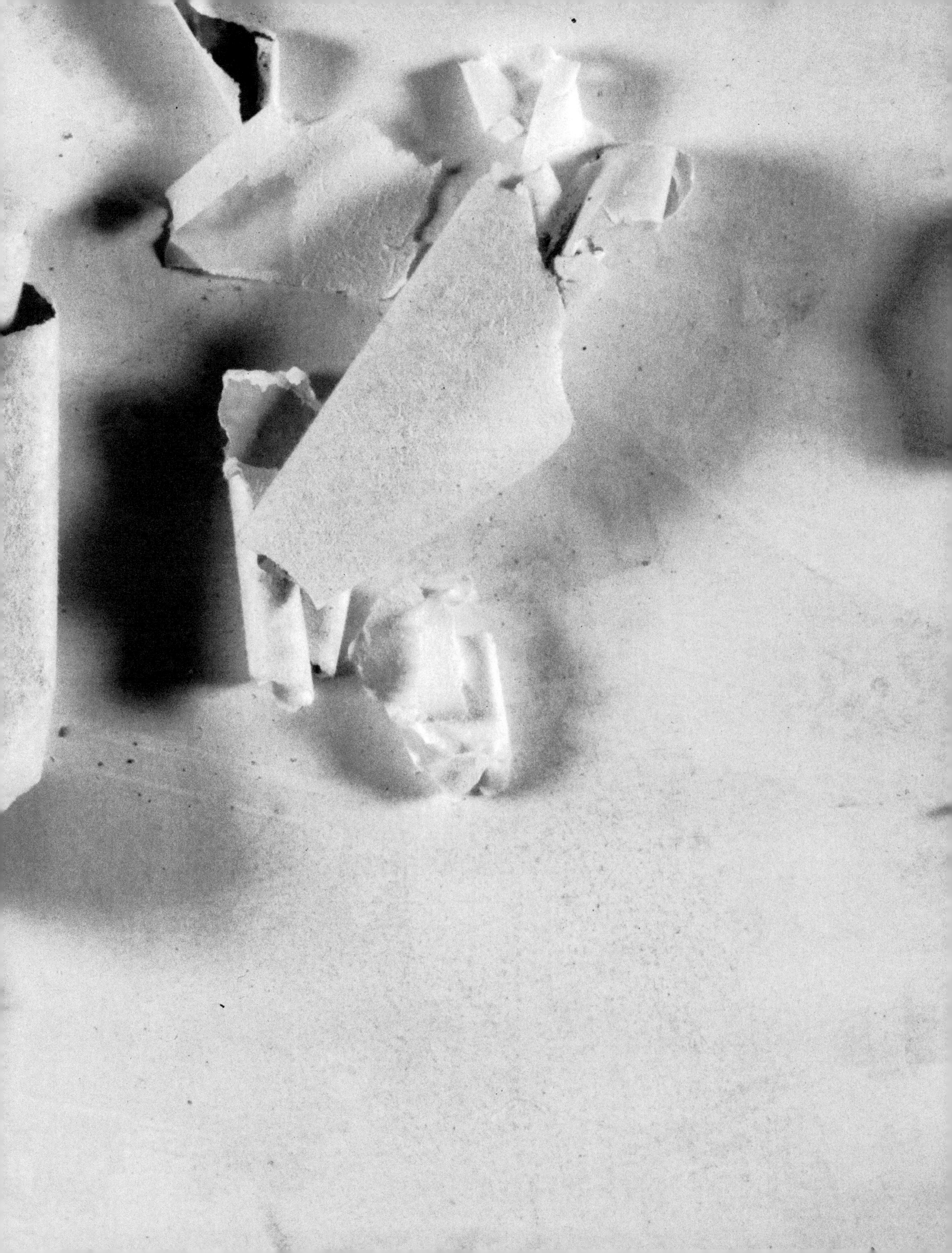

Prelude

I open the book on page 7 and slide the loose sheets off to the side. Sheets, printed in Lüneburg, several have visible watermarks, such imperfections drawing me closer to the reflective wall surfaces. I bypass the shadow of an absent figure and follow the lines of the window contours, resting my thoughts on the dimples of a domesticated concrete wall. Upon closer inspection those supposed imperfections, apparent indentations, appear to be a careful splatter of cement droplets.

Loose sheets, now being used as bookmarks as I continue reading. Drugstore sepia cast, a touch-screen icon, instantly offering a desired sheen to compliment the family album timeline. Train tickets and timeline piercings, furthermore-fixations; a couple of sepia prints, both overexposed and unsharp, a shard of shrink-wrap and a book, containing several short stories I wrote earlier this year. Since receiving the book last month it had been kept in shrink-wrap. Perhaps due to a reluctance to open, to confront and continue with this story, which is in its seventh year of transformation. Over the years the story's axis steadied, and became feather-light, but remained just as resolute and evasive as when first spoken.

Hahn / Huhn

I open the window outwards, occasionally there is sunlight and a view beyond. Beneath the window the S-Bahn passes by, but the view is centred by a hand holding a train ticket to the skyline. An attempt to articulate an oral story. It started while at art school, I wrote a short story as my historical studies dissertation. Years later, without realising the recurrence of location and narration, I travelled to Berlin, to search again for certain origins. To search for the evidence of a particular man, who once stood by a landmark, asking daily for the verification of identities. The remnants of the once biggest train station in Europe in the Nineteenth Century, just a façade still standing in 1945; his marker and our collective demarcation. I found the artifice, yet as for my man, all that was left standing and undisputed, was a kiosk in a grit-gravelled car park. A fat plastic chicken balancing, twisting. Its headless frame pivoting on the roof, the smell of roasted chicken pungently supplying a car park. According to the story, he ruminated by a kiosk, while being served coffee under a stirring sky. The kiosk was unmoved, it faced the façade, the last of the Anhalter Bahnhof. After years of telling the same story, only a few images remain pertinent to this day. I rotate a few sheets scattered on page 11 and set aside a loose image. My thoughts return to the book completed a few months ago.

I reach for the aforementioned loose sheet, previously set aside. An image taken at night: tyre tracks well set, compressed pristinely into the mud and hardened over time. A wordless billboard, stripped of its integrity and perspex panels, lit the brazened car park – located beside the grand station. A station devised for world domination, but derailment. The markings continue to hold an impression. Prior to the Second World War a swimming pool was planned by Albert Speer. The station always intended to stop. To reach the terminal before the destination, before the war. The train lines to stop short of the grand façade.

The mud markings were photographed just before I came across an entertainment complex, the Tempodrom – its apex centred on my view-finder, a new fixture depicted for the telling of this story. Leisure and post-modernity stylised into the framing of this centrefold image; the contemporary backdrop receding behind a façade. One which was 101-metres wide and crowned by two figurines, known as Day and Night. They were zinc clad, ionised, fallen markers. Day, on the right, was gazing into the distance, while Night, on the left, looked away.

A collection of images from the journey in 2003 still belong; regardless of whether they are printed, affixed to a wall, torn apart, taken down, shards collected, overlaid. Forgotten steps: wooden slabs, shattered Berliner Kindl shards ascending to the apex of the entertainment complex. Rows of monolithic plant pots, plastic vegetation, a systematic encumbrance. Such images became my navigational markers for time and company while strolling the pavements of my fabricated realities.

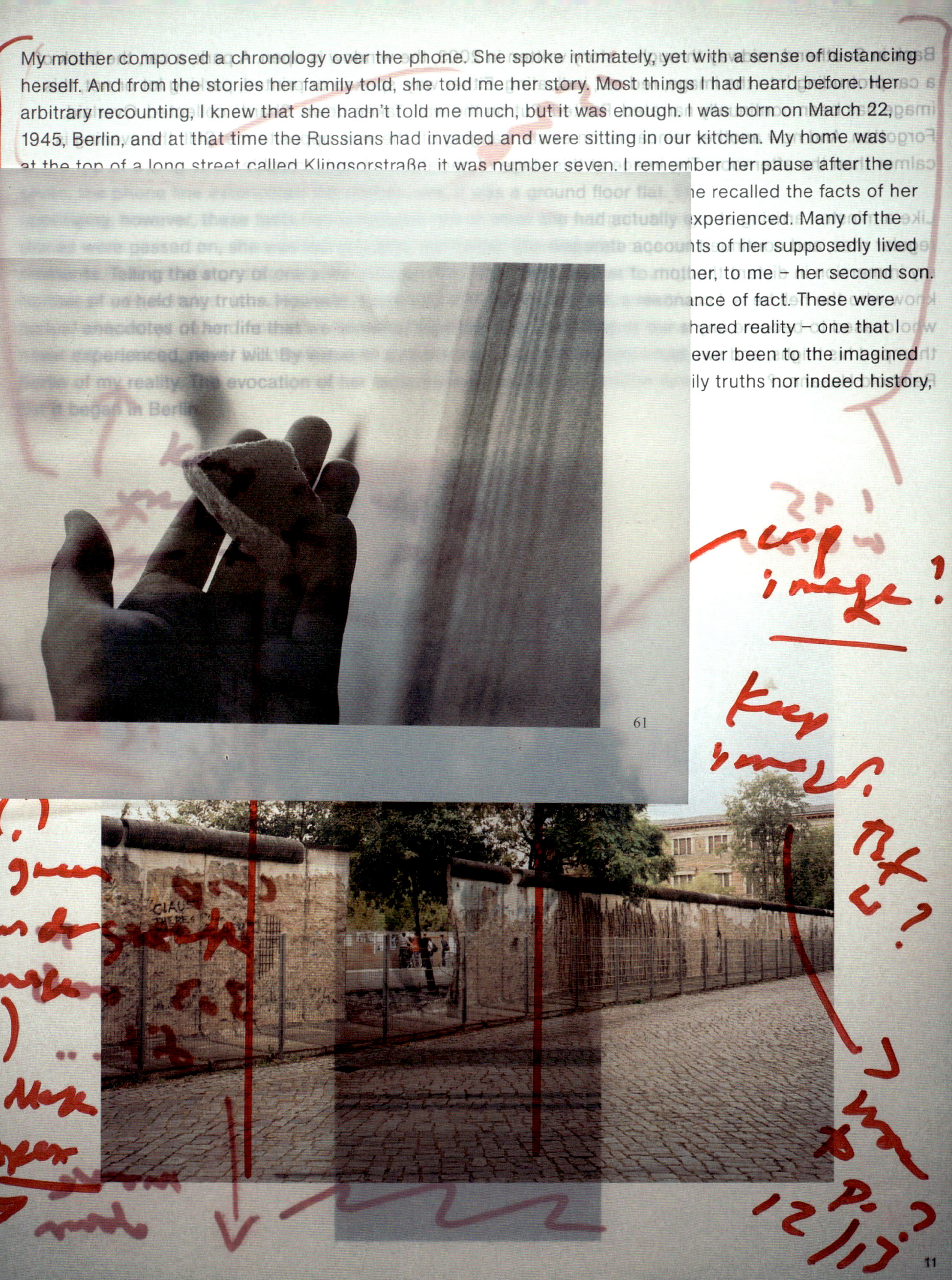

My mother composed a chronology over the phone. She spoke intimately, yet with a sense of distancing herself. And from the stories her family told, she told me her story. Most things I had heard before. Her arbitrary recounting, I knew that she hadn't told me much, but it was enough. I was born on March 22, 1945, Berlin, and at that time the Russians had invaded and were sitting in our kitchen. My home was at the top of a long street called Klingsorstraße, it was number seven. I remember her pause after the ... she recalled the facts of her ... experienced. Many of the ... accounts of her supposedly lived ... to mother, to me – her second son. ... ance of fact. These were ... hared reality – one that I ... ever been to the imagined ... ily truths nor indeed history,

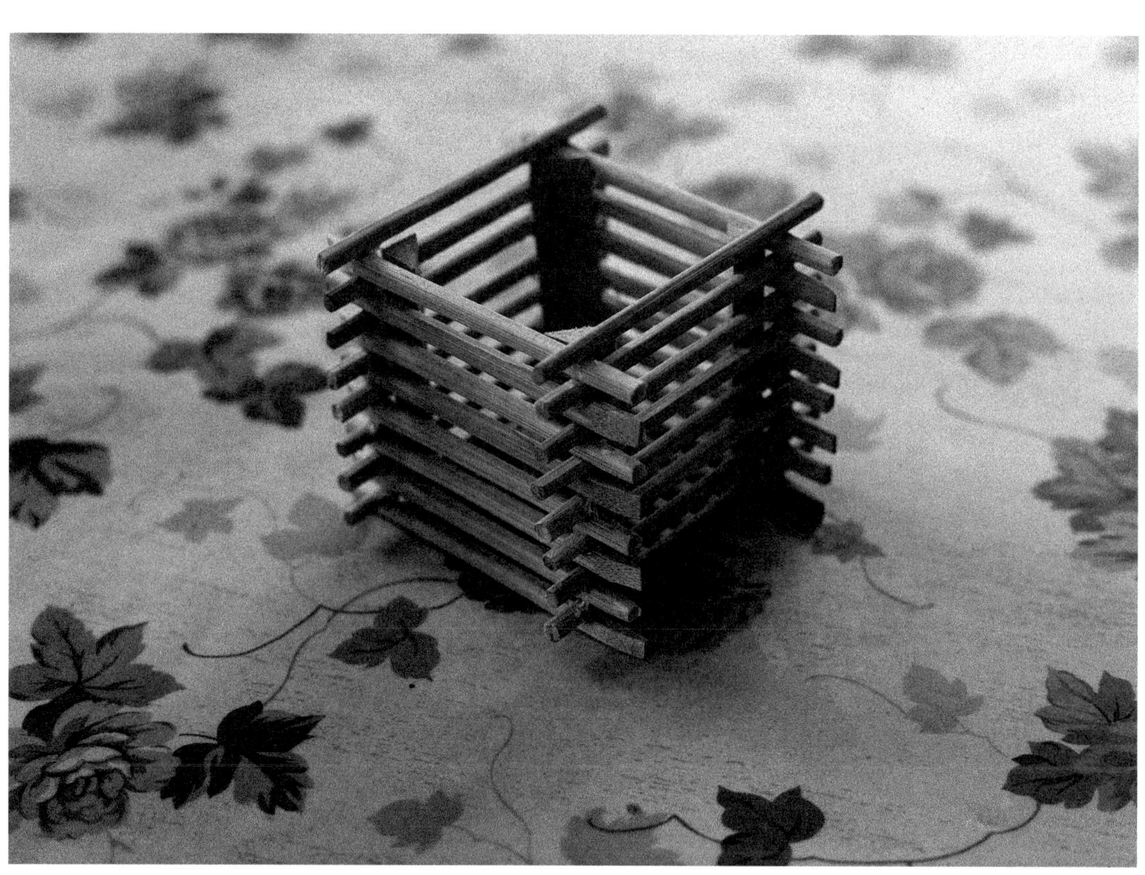

My first research trip to Berlin was during the spring time; I decided to sleep out each night, to be nocturnal. During the evenings I would search for water fountains to pass the twilight hours, hoping to find trickling water features with dissolving light units. During the mornings I would promenade along the canal and veer off into the undergrowth, covering platform sections and railway lines.

One afternoon as I crossed the canal, I noticed an underpass with weeds growing in all directions; since I hadn't slept well for the past few nights I decided to rest there. I fell asleep with my face to the ground and back bare. The whole day was spent laying below the U-Bahn lines between Gleisdreieck and Möckernbrücke. As the sun began to fall I stirred from my sleep, it was getting late so I headed northwards back into my encapsulated city of sheen and grid structure where the shallow pools of commerce caught the reflections of marketing brands, inverted wordings and shimmering lights.
I began photographing benches and passageways at dusk, elevators and entrances of inter-connected enterprises; these became the detailed familiar partitions for an inhabited space and bygone era. I ate an apple by a fountain, dropped the core in the water and spent hours watching it float its way in passive motions. Subtly lit, but just enough to photograph the journeying apple core until the early morning.

I discard a loose sheet on page 13 and continue reading the text beside it. Like a minstrel arriving at night, during the depleted hours of my concentration, my father summoned his regular rites, and continued his epic tale. Dancing within the rigid doorframe, until a recurring name broke my immersion in distant thoughts. You keep talking about him, but I keep forgetting who he is. I still don't know who the hell he is. I could sense that he enjoyed the outburst. The continual repletion of a figure who ceased to become any more available or comprehensive over time. Tension broken by laughter, he thumped his thighs, and swung the door in all directions, hailing, who is Reinhold Haahn... Haha... Who is Reinhold Haaahn...?

After August 13, 1961, the Anhalter Bahnhof functioned in the West sector of Berlin, but the S-Bahn was run by the East German government. Reinhold Huhn was one of many guards situated beneath the Anhalter Bahnhof, controlling the expansive underground tunnels. A few weeks prior to my departure for Berlin, there was a fire, causing the closure of the station for over a year. The façade still standing, scaffolds surrounding. I stood on the sand of my chosen place, and wandered to the next plot.

A transition from barbed wire to concrete to plastic. A moment, 1962. Reinhold Huhn stands there by the train station asking for papers, papier, documents. He's shot, and then, they say perfect, the GDR, they love it. The SED, they say, yes, we have a man who dies for communism, a man against capitalism. From barbed wire to concrete. Now concrete, a wall, a division. Reinhold Huhn, a 21-year old East German border guard, shot dead by a West Berlin escape agent on June 18, 1962. The Communist party commemorates him as a hero in the fight against the West. A pretext for furthering the perfection of the border system.

A school was erected in memory of Reinhold Huhn, and a monument ensued. Reinhold-Huhn-Straße existed. He gained cult status in the GDR and the authorities were eager to exploit his death for their political goals. There was little evidence that a monument ever stood, although I located where Reinhold-Huhn-Straße might have been – now named Schützenstraße. I wanted an image of the street sign, from above – an overview, a conclusive image to put it all in perspective. My only souvenir, a chink of spray-painted rubble: found, hand-held and photographed, depicted and printed on a loose sheet of paper, formerly a marker between words, between these words, but now a loose association, another fleeting image.

I flew out with two maps of Berlin, before and after the fall of the wall; according to the unified street map, Schützenstraße was a short distance away from where I sat, opposite a Jeff Koons sculpture placed in a stagnating pool of water. Further down on the same street, the Daimler AG tower stood – new heights. An elevator, with security guard nods. The button pressed. Incessant imagery unfurled from beyond the elevated cuboid space. I avoided eye contact, and took hold of the regulations board, inhaling the scent of slightly perfumed new tyres. Chrome walls, scratched. Upwards and onwards – exit – bing – doors opening – guests gone.

I switched my audio recorder on: HOLD-off to REC-on. As I approached the door the security guard wavered another nod, but then stopped in his stride, with one leg in and the other leaning out, he reached into his blazer pocket. The doors lingered, the elevator silence overriding the multi-medial scopes of dancing floral displays on the twentieth floor. Eventually his trailing leg released the jarred door, shut. He smiled, looked me up and down; I acknowledged his interpretation of my misinterpretation of this perceived world. He knew I wanted to capture something; an elevator ting perhaps, broken only by his intervention. Or a photograph, misplaced by my orientation. He continued the ascendancy, I withdrew my audio recorder. The elevator paused its trajectory, while he informed me of the regulations of the building, of the implications of capturing an image – in such a place, space.

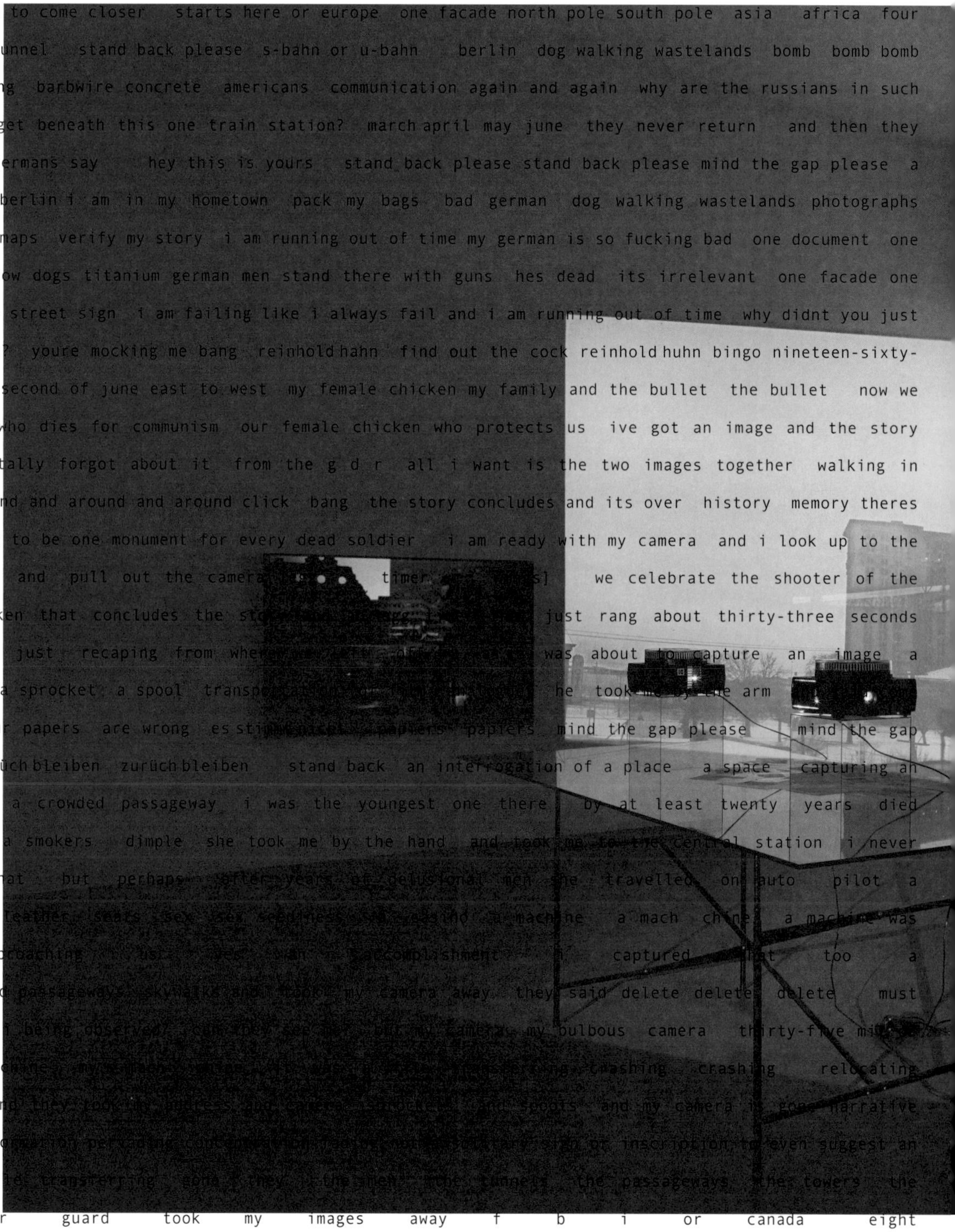

so if we are at five-forty-one and i will try to perform a piece relating to berlin if you cant hear me feel free to come closer starts here or europe one facade north pole south pole asia africa four buses one tunnel stand back please s-bahn or u-bahn berlin dog walking wastelands bomb bomb bomb bang bang bang barbwire concrete americans communication again and again why are the russians in such a hurry to get beneath this one train station? march april may june they never return and then they stop the germans say hey this is yours stand back please stand back please mind the gap please a story from berlin i am in my hometown pack my bags bad german dog walking wastelands photographs photographs maps verify my story i am running out of time my german is so fucking bad one document one photograph now dogs titanium german men stand there with guns hes dead its irrelevant one facade one monument one street sign i am failing like i always fail and i am running out of time why didnt you just go on google? youre mocking me bang reinhold hahn find out the cock reinhold huhn bingo nineteen-sixty-two twenty-second of june east to west my female chicken my family and the bullet the bullet now we have a man who dies for communism our female chicken who protects us ive got an image and the story ends i totally forgot about it from the g d r all i want is the two images together walking in circles around and around and around click bang the story concludes and its over history memory theres always meant to be one monument for every dead soldier i am ready with my camera and i look up to the street sign and pull out the camera timer [camera clicks] we celebrate the shooter of the female chicken that concludes the story that alarm just rang about thirty-three seconds ago hello just recaping from where was about to capture an image a photograph a sprocket a spool transp he took me by the arm with me your papers are wrong es stimmt nicht papers papers mind the gap please mind the gap please zurück bleiben zurück bleiben stand back an interrogation of a place a space capturing an image in a crowded passageway i was the youngest one there by at least twenty years died black hair a smokers dimple she took me by the hand and took me to the central station i never requested that but perhaps after years of delusional men she travelled on auto pilot a comfort a feather seats sex user seeing casino a machine a mach chine a machine was fast approaching us man accomplishment i captured it too a space crowded passageway skywalks and took my camera away they said delete delete delete must remove am i being observed? can they see? but my camera my bulbous camera thirty-five mill aps my machine my machine crashing crashing relocating relocating and they took my images and scoots and my camera is gone narrative rupture information per sign or inscription to even suggest an ending file transferring and they the tunnels the passageways the towers the grenze border guard took my images away f b i or canada eight mile concrete barbwire bullet stand back please your papers blue print as memory they were fast approaching me www dot ed com de it corrupted window panels and childhood friends wood chip and mexican town the drone goes on but confusion prevails crashing relocating relocating data transferral they took my camera   delete   delete   delete   infringing windows and childhood friends   am i being   observed? i dont know what she wanted or who or why   i or he a machine   a machine a machine death crashing   crashing a twilight   death dead   a machine a lover a love a lover   or   him or he   am i being observed? i wanted to capture something a monument   a document a   verification of a story a journey a monument for my dead solider but where? www dot com de   dot de dot it   or org dot   org   yes an accomplishment   an accomplishment   black   blue   a photograph yes i remember capturing that too   a man in echoed dia in echoed   dialogue i remember capturing that too i thought it an omen   you too?   in circles avec movais francais or   german asking for my one dead solder to verify a journey   a monument   astro turf and football pitches in berlin   dog walking wastelands and a station eighteen-eighty-eight or eighteen-eighty-two   the dates change repetition   relocating   crashing   crashing but i remember   yes an omen   the sta station   eighteen stories   high   up   a station   biggest in eighteen-eighty-two in europe europe or berlin epicentre   of europe detroit in america   eighteen stories up high dog walking wastelands   i wanted one document one   monument   one image   capturing that too yes an accomplishment a piece of marble   abricated noises of landscape and infringing windows security guards f b i glass panels fixtures postdammer platz   jeff koons   centre epi   epicentre of berlin   dog walking wastelands   eighteen   stories   up   high   snow foot prints   am i being observed?   can   she   see   me?   delete   delete   the   infringing windows   thunder twilight animals   empty traces foot prints and microphones in your ears   am i being observed? i have no idea   i a machine   she   travelled on auto pilot central station eighteen stories up high eighteen-eighty-two berlin or detroit u s a   or canada   a border   a   a division and moment in time and history   documenting a grenze   division grenze   guard and or security guard   currents of rain water perform their way across the large window large glass panes   echoed dialogue empty passageways so crowded yet empty   so empty yet crowded with childhood friends   a machine a mach chine   a despondent alarm clock   a struggling water boiler nearby my mouth is dry im struggling to keep the pace i realise its impossible to tell you this story in yes   a struggling water boiler nearby   churning heavily i cant   go on i need a break half way through   im lost   lost the track   the needle on the player   the record   it got caught well i got caught   trying to document and experience a city so devoid of people and experiences   unless you chose to insert yourself   within   a   construct   and   be there   comfort leather seats this city this place   is always beyond me and every time i tried to capture something in this place   it took me elsewhere in front of this large picture of a past every time place and ending   relocating i think how i will take a quick break and return in five or seven minutes   i realise a work whose title ceases to exist to maintain to stay the same   but im bypassing   you are bypassing   im struggling my mouth is dry   stagnating water   and a despondent alarm clock   ground thuds and mesmerising water patterns my eyes catch the public   after this break of a about five or seven minutes   back soon thank you

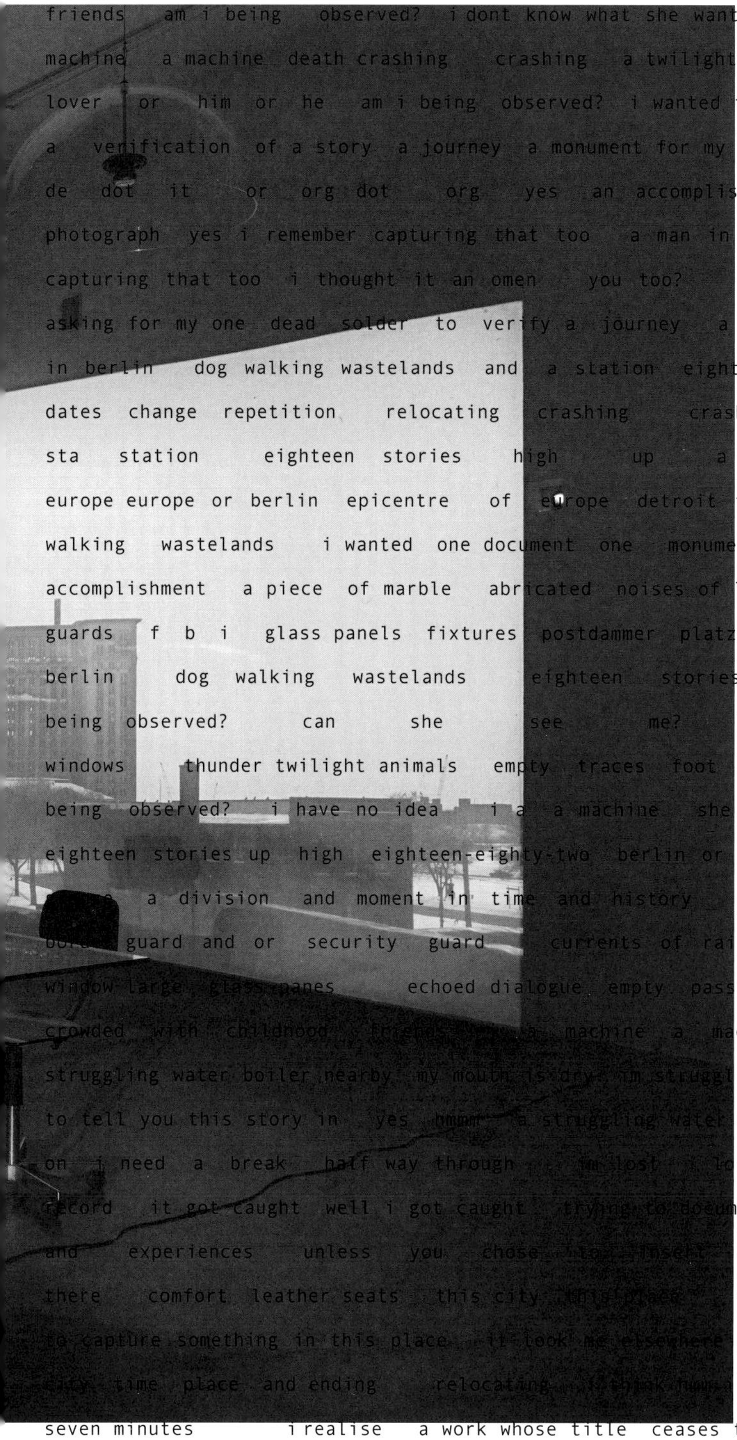

Interlude

I stood between three pin boards on Easter Sunday at 6:30 pm, and performed the piece I could not escape. A performance scheduled to take place between six and eight and to last between seven and twelve minutes. Such time parameters, still insignificant. Although I needed a framework, since I knew that the images, whether sheets or slides, would soon lose their meaning. Seven or twelve minutes, time would still escape me. I completed the story one or two seconds prior to the maximum time slot of twelve minutes. The egg-timer rang as I concluded, seldom has that happened during a performance.

Conversely the accompanying images hindered the spoken narration and threw me off track, off balance yet on time. It ended, the egg timer rang – yet the destination not quite there. I conceded that the story I knew too well and have performed over a hundred times had begun to distill. It was the first time since I wrote the words in 2003 that I performed the story in such a way – with the aid of pin boards for makeshift meaning and orientation. I was lost in a familiar world. I saw the sheets daily during the install, held and sequenced the same few slides for several years and performed the core narratives forever longer.

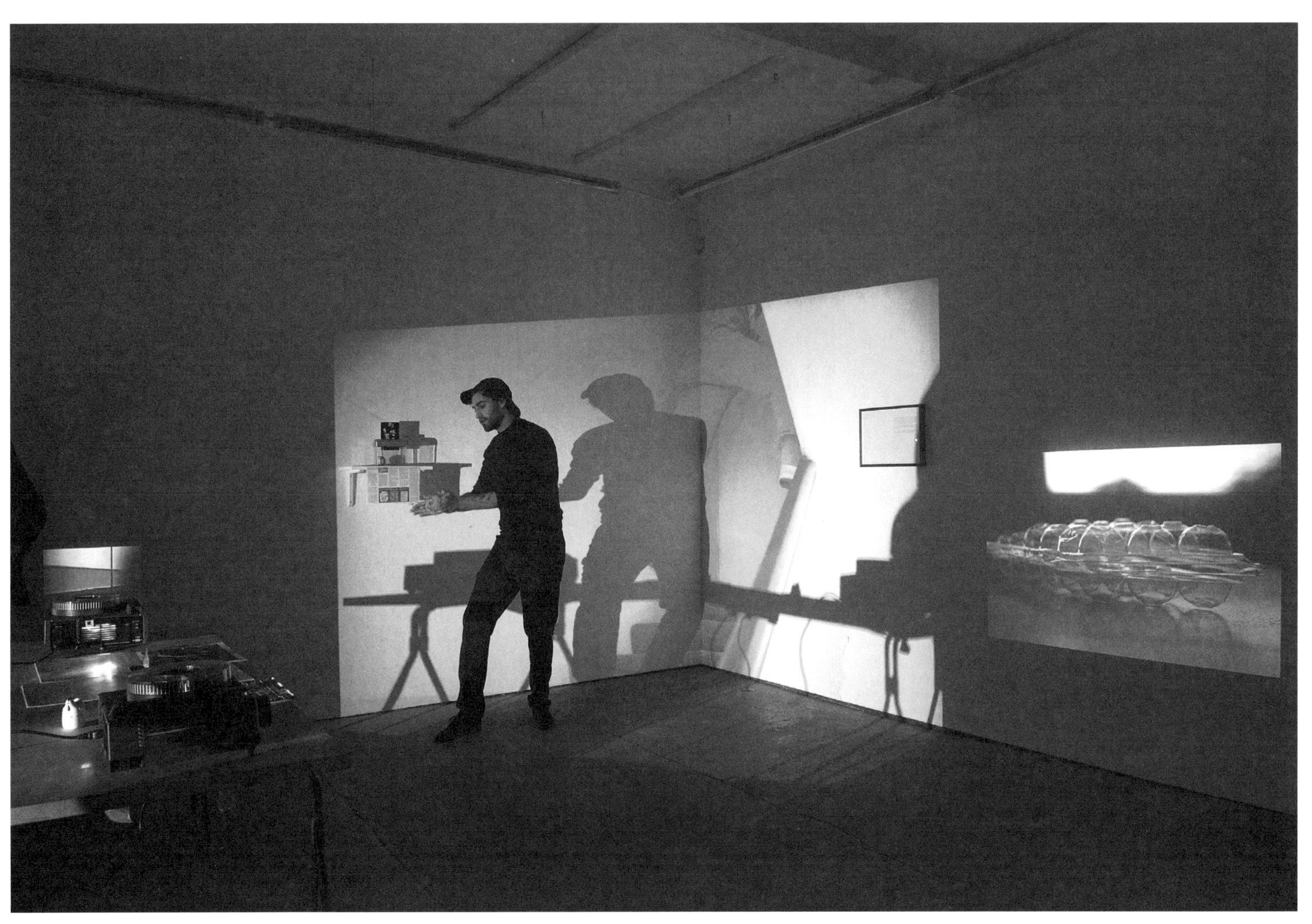

Leipzig Calendar Works

The year was 2005, and the intention was to spend a few days in Berlin, before heading down to Leipzig. A starting point: Stasi archives which evaded the electric shredder or furnace during the final days of the GDR, only the hand-torn shards remaining to this day. And in Zirndorf, thirty-one Puzzlers are reconstructing the documents from millions of shards. Mr Raillard points at the page, these are the figures for forty workers, he says. As you see, we only have thirty-one.

I transported my archive of childhood photographs to Germany in a relish green suitcase, which had a painful handle. Hundreds of photographic prints, a few strips of uncut negatives, a mini paper shredder and two tweezers surrounded me. I had an additional bag full of adhesives and calendars. My plan for Leipzig was to shred and collate uninterruptedly for one month in a GDR MDF Bedroom. It had light, three windows, MDF furniture and hundreds of photographs covering the laminate flooring. In 1989 a Peaceful Revolution took place outside this bedroom, the janitor nonchalantly informed me upon my arrival. After a few days, three photographic categories expanded across the floor: glossy photographs in Ferrero Rocher chocolate boxes, and lustre and matt photographs in separate envelopes. The shredder often clanked, perpetually jammed. A shutter.

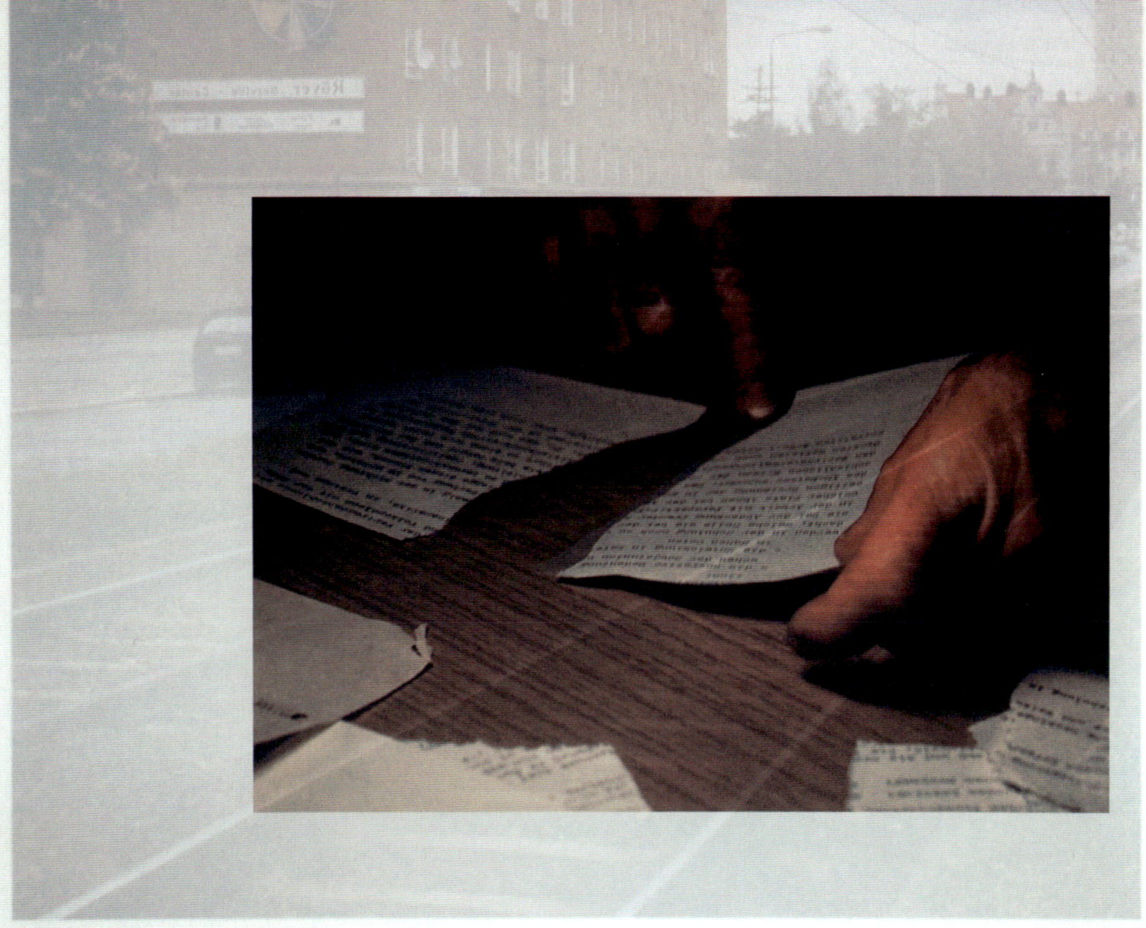

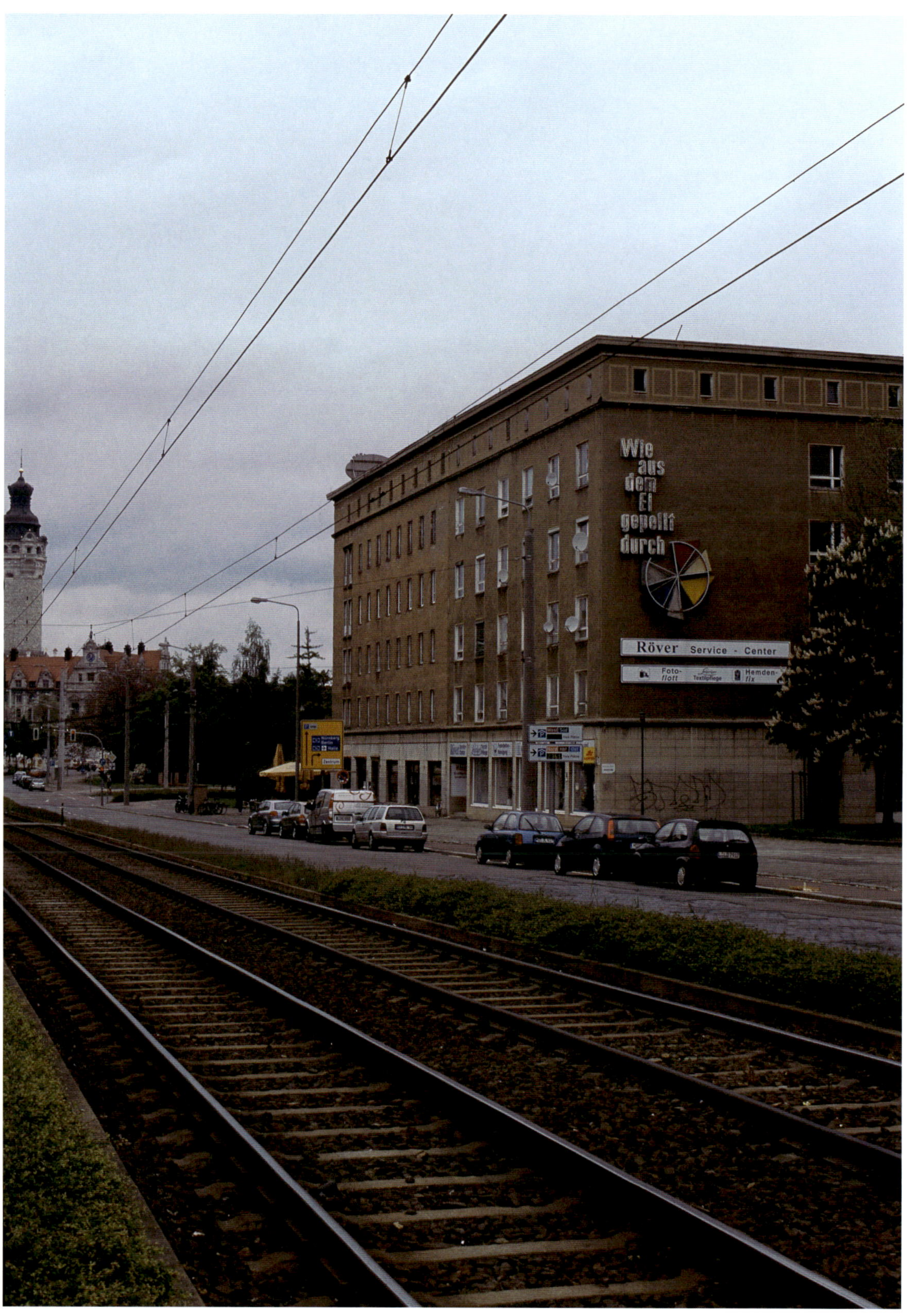

Wie
aus
dem
Ei
gepellt
durch
Röver Service - Center
Foto-flott
Textilpflege
Hemden-fix

im cutting im cutting im tearing im tearing cut cut cut tear tear tear cut cut
tear tear and the photographs have been decanted and the photographs
from april first from dick und doof to may   to may day to june from van
gogh and shutters left and right and im shredding and its almost over   may
day may day and then its done from one month in solitude   and they shred
shred shred and they shred and their machines massive machines i have a
small machine they have a big machine   they have papers millions hundreds
of millions of papers and they shred shred shred shred shred and bang
exposure too many too many files

im sh-sh-shredding and im shredding im shredding and im collaging im
collaging and tweezers and pritt sticks and calendars calendars and the stasi
and they shred shred shred with machines and bang and they say shit and
they cut and they cut and they tear eighty-nine october november december
revolution they say shit and they cut and they say no no   burn   let them
burn   all over east germany moment in time from leipzig to villages to
berlin to stasi   smoke   synchronicity left right   smoke   and the east
germans say   why is there synchronicity

in this city to the village to east germany to this moment in time   smoke
pillars   pillars synchronicity revolution   they say wonderful and the stasi
stasi they flee they flee they burn   the c i a   the men the men they collect
the lines the shapes the papers the forms the forms   and they piece them
together and they take them away   and all thats left now is this   in a room
with an egg timer with four minutes left   from the shredding from the april
to the may to the june and now its complete   perfect

While shredding and collating photographic shards over used calendars, I started to devise my exit.
The day after May Day, I departed for Paris with a suitcase containing thousands of torn and shredded
photographs, and three newly collated calendars: April, Liverpool F.C. calendar from 1998, of which
the pictorial lines of a football player I never knew were pasted over; May, Vincent van Gogh calendar,
The Bedroom, completed in Arles, 1888, selected and left untouched, the punctum; June, ART of the
Twentieth Century, 2000, Women Running on the Beach, 1922, the departure.

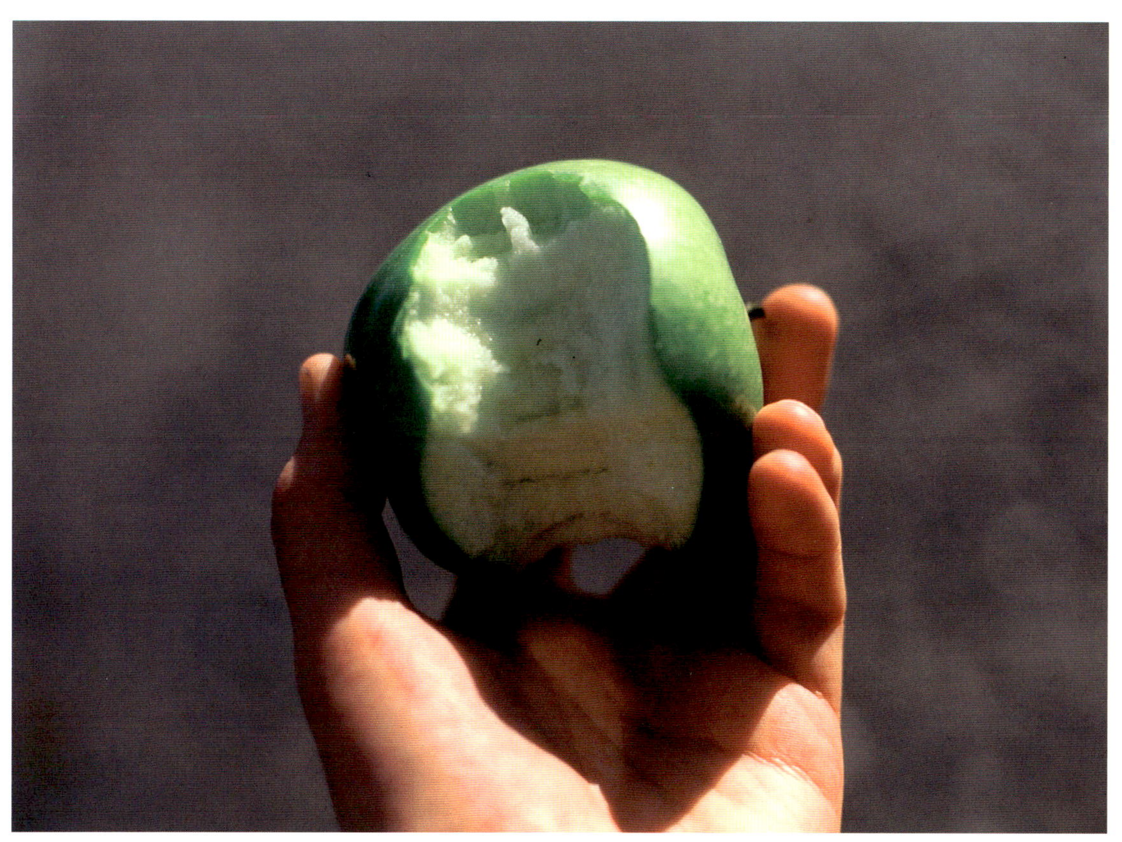

Finding Chopin

Before leaving Southend for Glasgow, I needed to visit the storage unit to collect materials for a performance scheduled for the following evening.

A secondary table placed beside me to aid the selection process. A lightbox plugged in, the first outpour of slides.

Where to start? A scatter of slides: Lisbon, a subtle rainbow, barely visible, rising up from a water fountain curb, chipped; British Columbia, the Motor Inn, kneeling on cold gravel at dawn; Rotterdam, a dark sky, an early morning lull by a partially lit war memorial; Den Haag, potato chips at dusk; an unknown home, with laminate flooring, corrugated radiator and a softened arm, holding pose, failing; Vancouver, open twenty-four hours, with neon lines, words plentiful, nightfall; theme park railing, golden spray. Another archive box opened: a white umbrella protruding from her waist, the handle propped against the back of a fellow passenger's chair; train tickets and timeline piercings, furthermore-fixations; images of plastic, shoes, canvas, cotton, legs. It was time to leave the storage unit, I pulled the metal shutters down and locked up. I was late for the airport bus.

good evening   i think   urm   [sound of a
lid being replaced on a water bottle] in this
circumstance   if   ah   no   no its fine
yeah   urm   so   i wonder if those at the
back can hear me   there   theres no um
amplification here   its just two microphones
for the context of a recording   as a way to
continue or expand or conclude this particular
work   called finding chopin   [breathes in]
which started in two-thousand-and-five and
usually   the story   it starts actually with
saying the lake district   and the   kind of
trajectory just flies off   but instead of
doing that i will just kind of introduce the
idea why theres actually only two chairs and
two ladies sitting here

The next morning I began to unpack, it was time
for slide sequencing and rehearsing. Selecting
slides for a verbal story, which long ago
ceased to welcome any new motifs. I took out
a collection of archive boxes from my bag: the
first box containing images of rubber bands,
wound up and disbanded; the smallest baggage
conveyor belt I'd ever seen, located and almost
discarded; followed by images of hotel desks,
windows, summers and silhouettes caught in the
act of observation; more images spreading across
the lightbox, markers, pens, porous surfaces,
slender arms, and time.

well   this narrative has come
to a point where   after years of
performing this piece   its very
difficult to   derail   that now
every time i try to perform it   i
know that if i see a particular
word it takes me there   and thats
somehow   a hinderance   but its
inevitability   it happened by the
fact of repetition   so this is
an attempt to uh   remove the slides
decant them   present this work in
this context   and hopefully uh
[leans across the table and switches
the projector off] keep it true to
its essence

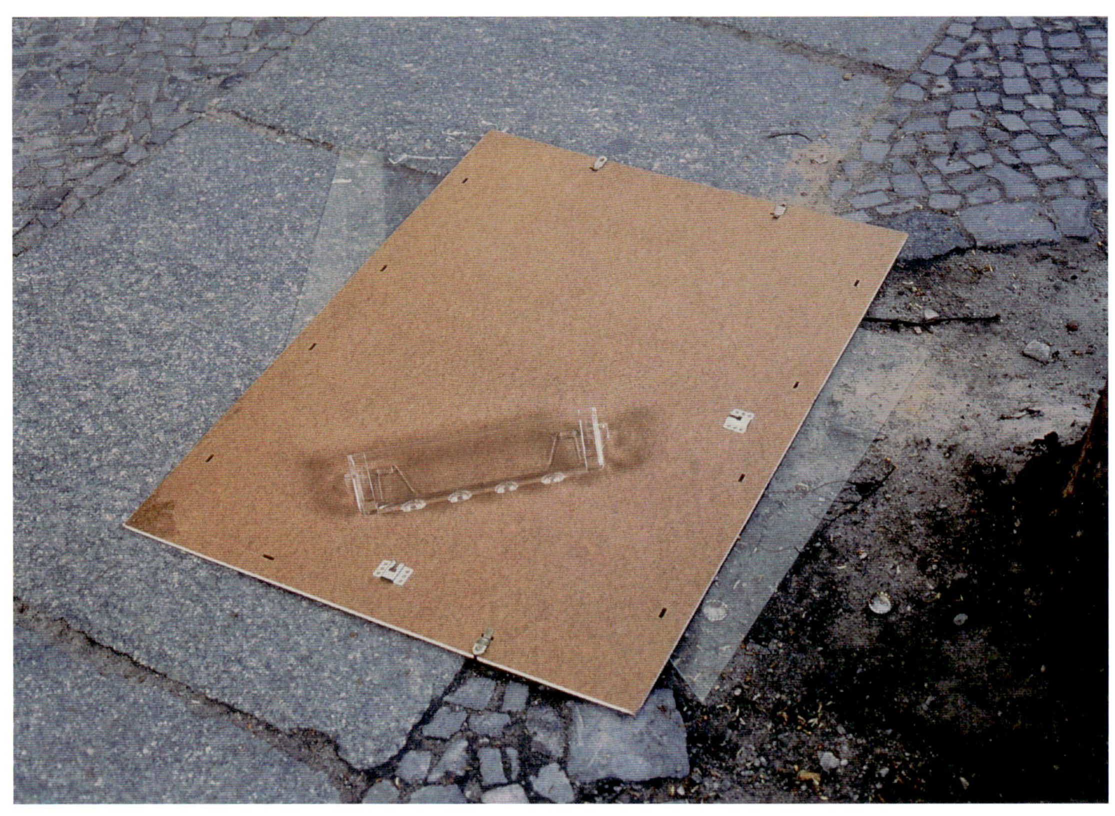

Certain motifs and associations still forming
and upholding the visual logic for this
work, I admit, for no apparent reason. Like
in a hotel room, trying to construct a visual
sequence to accompany a loosely bound story.
Besides, I've used certain images since
the beginning; intuitively stored in vague
categories, none sufficiently labelled to
suggest any unity. For example these here:
pictures of fabric or paper wrapped around
poles, pipes, or the pier in Southend.

When travelling I often hope for such
pictorial arrangements, by now I have a whole
collection of these images. Somehow they became
undercurrent images for the Chopin narrative,
yet they were intended to function as a
narrative of form. Usually they would run behind
me in an abstract way.

Performing the same
narratives, unfolding and
rotating, again and again and
again. The story's content is
digressing, losing its hold
and moving on.

More images, the origins of the work, existing only to inform the spoken word. But now, after five years of repetition, speech has developed beyond these references. Blank slides can exist. Gradually images started declining, in the sense of carrying an affirmative reason for existence, in terms of a sequence. Simultaneous to the disintegration of certain images, the objects I had collected began entering the frame. A new vocabulary started to develop – as words, as images, interlocking and replacing pre-existent forms. A much needed transition, regardless whether the objects themselves forged new relationships.

Every image could be explained in the sense of origins, where it was shot, why it was created, and what the intended connotations were. But I can't keep track of such origins, since the images continue to find new references, forms and meaning. The presence of an audience – acceleration, adrenaline, both inducing a transformation of materiality into something visceral, inconsistent, and aloof from an intended meaning. I recognise this slide, it was used from the very beginning; the number seven burnt into the flesh of a yellow pepper. Back then, I believed that the story should be seven minutes. No longer, no less.

But, as the narratives developed, and as I continued to expand the speech, seven was never enough – was always inadequate, it just sounded good. And in the purity of words without images, without objects, the story suffered. Eventually the story began to balance out, symbolism made way for new meanings.

so   i have an egg timer and um   i often do say to the two people sitting here   you can decide the duration but then again   of course   its just two peoples opinions out of twenty-two or twenty-three   but nonetheless time   always works   because   it keeps me in tune with what im supposed to say or not say   i would always recommend between seven and twelve   um   seven makes it pretty fast   twelve is just enough information   beyond twelve   i start to lose my voice [murmur of laughter from audience] and   um actually underneath seven   it means its a lot more abstract   but i think its up to you two to decide

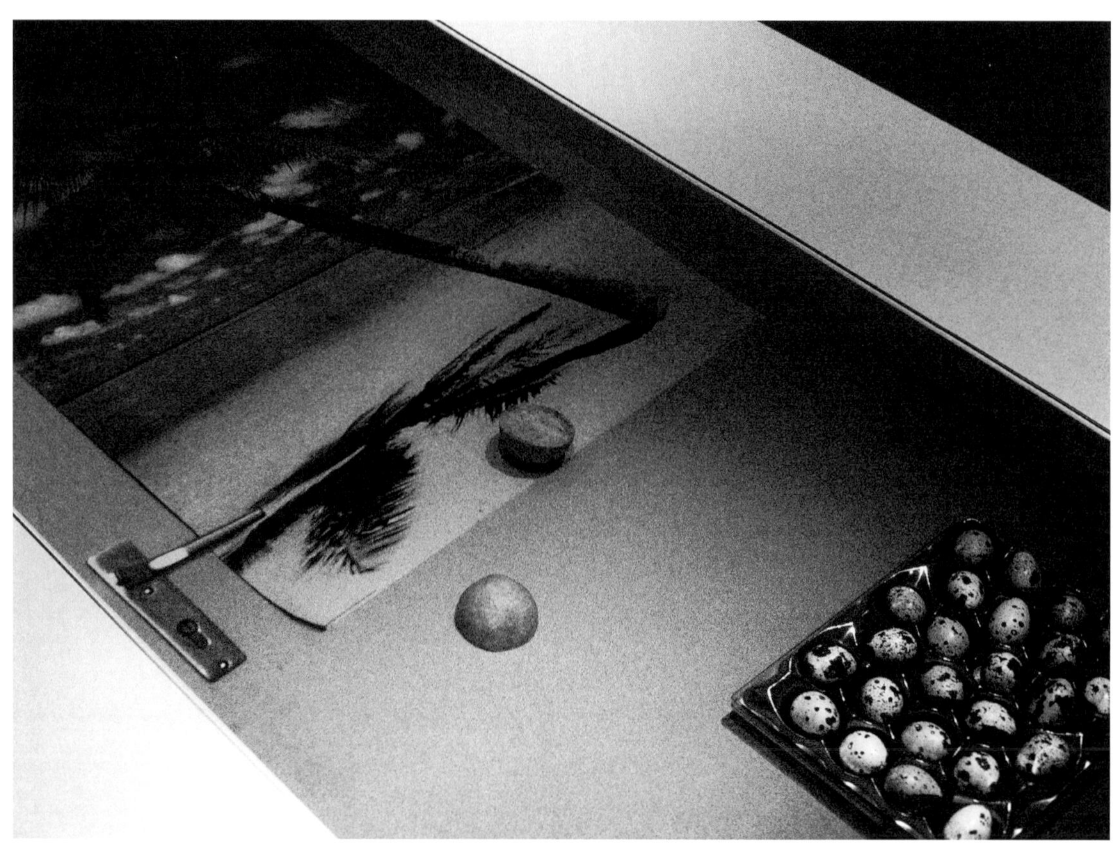

Eighty slides now systematically arranged on my desk, although probably thirty of them are images from another narrative; of government officials working in Zirndorf, near Nuremberg.

Like this image here: of an archival tape ball, there's a cohesion of narratives fracturing and merging the whole, constantly. The Puzzlers, as they were called, kept adhering to the whole; and in the end, a few byway balls of production, circular and still expanding, remain within my grasp. It's impossible to narrate consistently, or to omit the Stasi chapter from the entirety of the Chopin narration.

also   um   most of the things that i
have now that were once props   are not
even relics but they actually ceased to
work   so it does say ten minutes   i hope
it will be ten minutes   but perhaps it
wont even ring   fifty percent of the time
it doesnt ring im not too sure   but the
story as always   it always starts in the
same place and i   [noise of an egg timer
being wound, ticking starts]   i actually
regret that it starts in the lake district
ambleside   and kurt schwitters   left or
right   lake district   trees   trees   a
museum   a pencil museum   a museum for
pencils   for lines   for shapes   colours
and forms   i   said wow   why is there
a museum of pencils   in the middle of
nowhere   and then   kurt schwitters   a
house   a little house or dormitory   an
old lady comes out and says   cup of tea
love   and the story starts every single
time in two-thousand-and-five   but i dont
want it to   but it always does   i walk in

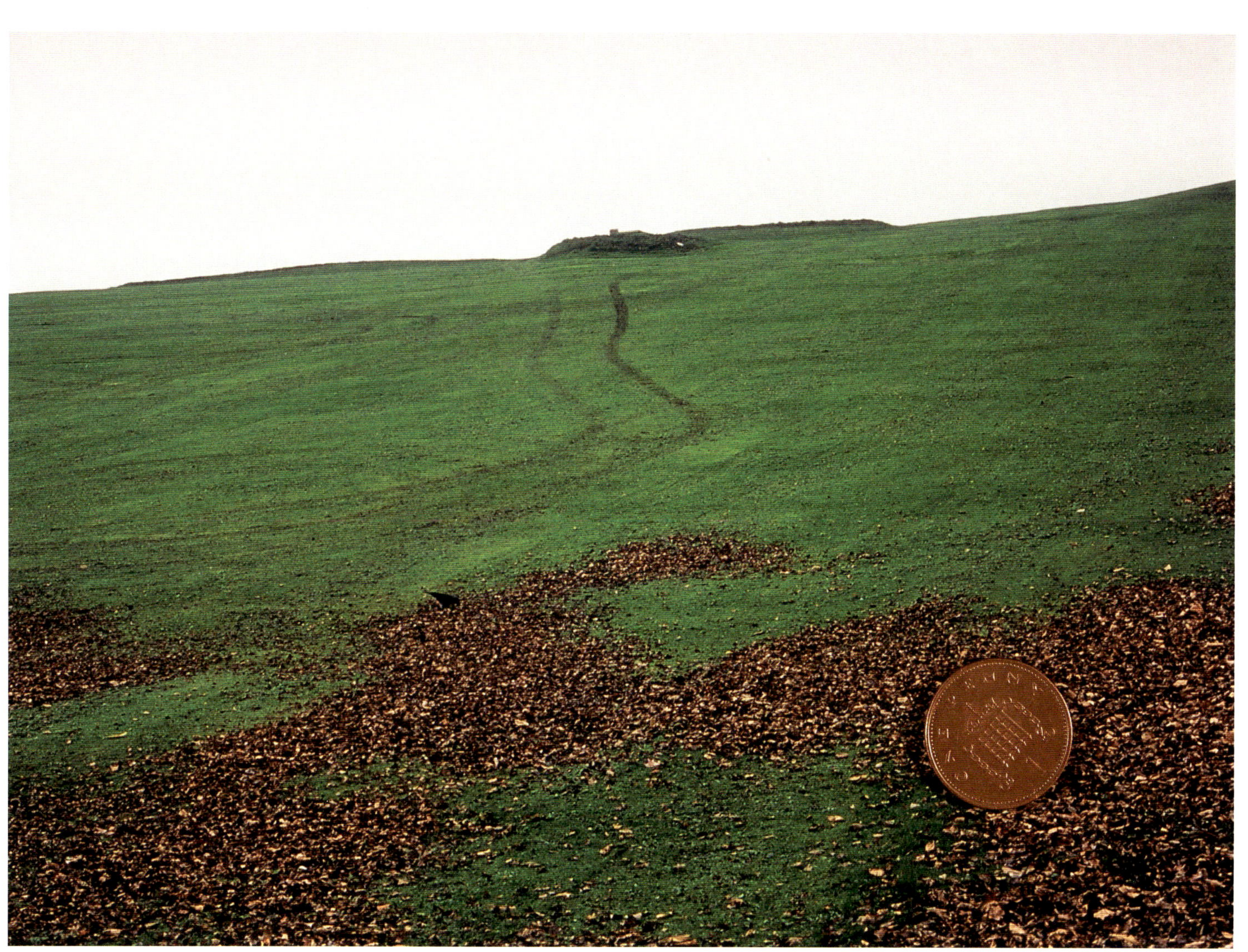

Wasteful Illuminations

I hoped that the narratives originating in 1888 or circling events in 1989 or memories of 2001 could all coexist – in one story, in a twelve minute performance or a montage of images. Last year I took a dozen carousels home from a photo lab, only six carousels contained slides. Two of which appeared to be of a father and son's holiday from the early Nineties. I selected the four other carousels and placed them beside a lightbox. They were reiterations of the same lecture, each carousel possessing a core set of images and distinct chronology. Recurring in different formations were blackboard slides. The only visible consistency on each board were minuscule piercings towards all four edges. It was an odd construct – imperfect, yet the ideal void for overlaying another image. A serrated border, somehow, was backlit by a sepia glow. What kind of an image did the creator envisage for such an enchanted backdrop? Was the intention simply to place the thirty-five-mil slide on a cutting mat and carve a window into existence – for a new slide to occupy the negative space?

In each varying carousel I realised that the slides followed a certain logic. These blackboard voids were the abstractions in the creator's narration. Aside from the abstract images, the rest were taken from printed sources, casting a factual tone and historical voice over most slides. A succession of discernible visual facts – speechless. Perhaps it was the first time I had held a slide which I considered historical. While slowly decanting each carousel only a few images enticed me beyond the actual enjoyment of ciphering through a discarded collection of slides. The found images didn't uphold an objective history, but so many images I had seen before, regularly throughout my life, and this new found familiarity with an antiquated technology and visual meaning brought me closer to the absent creator than words could have done. The last slide from the final carousel, all four had been emptied. I was unsure of how many hours had passed by while sifting through carousels. I rounded up the slides relating to the lectures and placed them in archive boxes, making way for a clean surface to accommodate a new set of narratives.

Electrical grillwork hangs from a concrete ceiling, spotlights and polystyrene tiles removed; now a dimly lit room. Slide projections, a shimmering water feature and narrow skylights determine the contours of the space. A sedentary clock, immovable and uninformative lays in close proximity. I look for my notes for this story, soon to be performed in a space still in transition. A soundtrack present, incessant cicadas. Safety boulders, square, or water fountains, circular, attempt to lay the framework for this refracted story.

One which starts on a bicycle; I worked at a sorting office, night shifts, induced by the need to supplement a hobby. I collected phone cards as a teenager and bred cold water fish. Moments, caught or fleeting; accumulating by a water feature, passive water ripples, illuminated by LED fixtures, passing time. And in-between the postal service job and the installing of an exhibition, a convenience store came into view on the other side of a dual carriageway. As I crossed the lanes, I hesitated on a traffic island, it was a meagre stretch of concrete – it appealed to me. An island, a vanishing point, and a convenience store supplying a variety of rice cakes. A slender slab continuing well beyond sight, fog and drowsiness convinced me to stay; it soon became my intimate space, located between a multitude of lanes and markers. I fell asleep amongst the swaying shrubbery, I felt safe there, besides, few would have expected to find someone taking refuge in such a place.

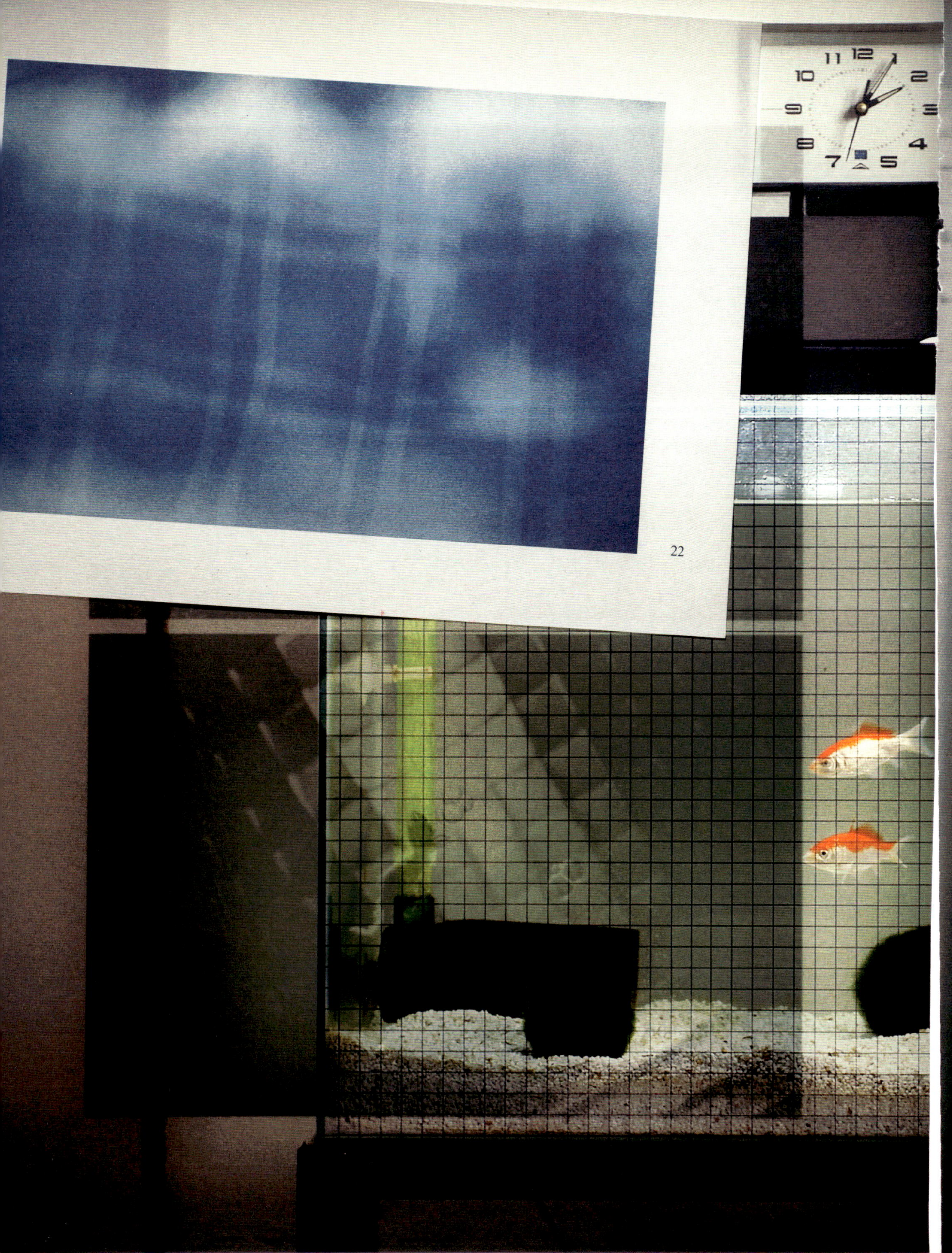

22

At dawn I was awoken by motorcycle engines. Rising from the flattened shrubs I saw a rally of masked bikers revved against a racing line. Due to my stupefied state I couldn't work out whether they were waiting for me, or for a signal above my head. It appeared they were all focused on a particular patch of land, precisely where I happened to lay. I looked up at my bag, which hung from a crooked sign post.

The information meant nothing to me, I was more interested in the slab of concrete, my island elevated off the asphalt tracks. I was safe there, invisible, I believed. Dressed in black, each biker was masked by a piece of white fabric, folded in a triangular fashion. Cleanliness, I held that image, a fitting image of domestic and urban form. Alloys or culinary folds, both gleaning for attention. I reached for my bag and dragged it into my enclosure; camera to my face, I started shooting in the dark. Nine years ago, while kneeling on that traffic island, the camera I held was broken – a jammed shutter and cracked mirror. The clanks of transportation deceived me, no image left its mark.

A circular metal pole, a construct and holding.

This fragment further displaced by a parallel image and an inserted sheet. Above the toilet seat, a slender marble sill presents a brittle flower, spruced. Elevators: articulated enclosures, continue to punctuate this story. A scented journey, in splendid pace – from the concourse landing to the sky-garden observatory the elevator journey elapsed in approximately forty-odd seconds.

Leaning on the railing, peering down from the sixty-ninth floor I began to photograph: a deviation from the monochromatic slants of an urban rooftop – my lens focusing on a lady, a portrait in the waiting, but I saw no other camera or companion so I took

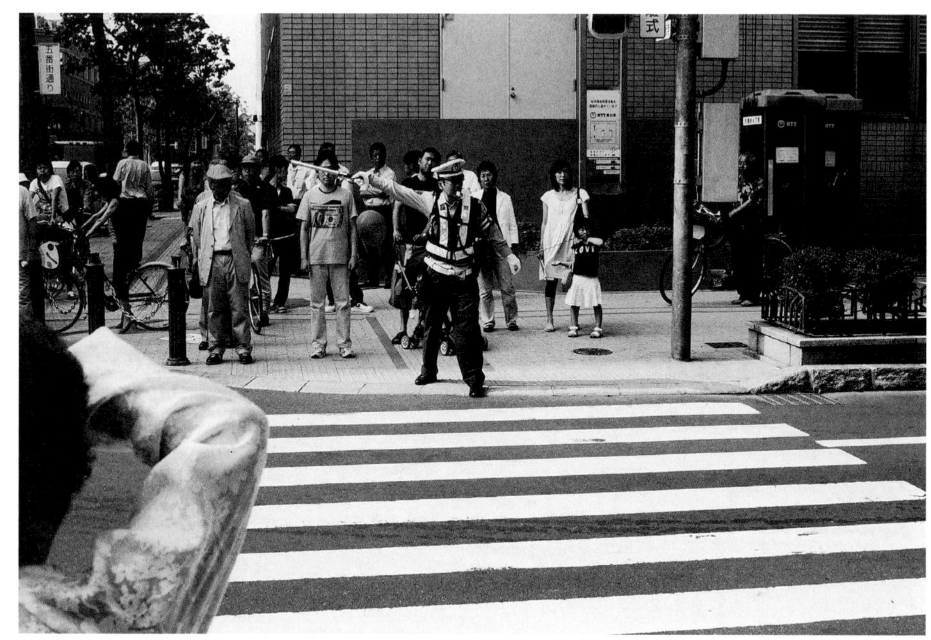

the liberty and sampled a few more gazes for my memory banks. Moving laterally on from her posed shoulders, images of the estuary banks, tarred rocks resurfacing. Splashes against the pavement. Brittle weeds growing upright between rocks and concrete. A windy day, shrubs swaying towards the left of the frame. An image of a marble expanse, aligned by metal trimmings. A hollowed bush. Void. Open. Closing. Flushing, I hold up the wooden flower ornament – and pick off a petal, my marker.

Returning to memories of estuary walks passing deformed bushes along the shoreline. Smoke. Burnt. Diversion. Fireworks and crackle, smack, pop – images of theme parks by an ever-shortening entertainment pier. Bumper cars and candy-floss, ever-faster collisions. Apologies, my usual greeting to the evening, but instead of commencing, thoughts of buggy-type machines, syntax memory loops from other over-arching shorelines or storylines impede any advancement.

I wish I knew how to rehearse, I would often curse. Still on the rooftop, but now in an interior space, a viewing platform – a sky lounge with window curvatures spanning three-sixty around floral displays of fabricated nature and highlife. Reflections of marketing brands from entertainment spaces, sky-top cafes, rotating views and inverted wordings. Introspection, the rustling of my shirt lapel as I try to steady the microphone. My eyes scan the objects on a nearby table. The necessary verities, all within my view, my grasp – such material confirmations belonging to a journey. The noncompliant co-ordinates of this brutalist space is all I have to project onto, hoping to conjure up a beginning.

Audience soon present, objects domicile and within reach. Non-projected images of benches and passageways at dusk prompt the opening line of thought. Elevators and entrances of a monolithic slab, concrete. Definitive. I place a red MiniDisk recorder on the glass table top and press the open switch, releasing the lid, a pop-up panel; an acknowledgment that the story is upon me. I will start by acknowledging the poor acoustics in the room and urge the audience to come closer – because, as always, there will be no amplification in this space, nor room for reverberation.

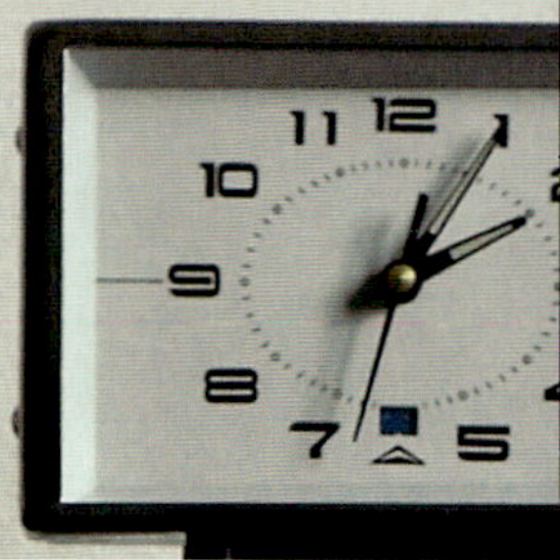

immense parentheses solitude inscriptions nothing delete delete   blank currents of noise muddling noise of data transfer   data referral they took my camera currents of rain water performing its way across the large window large glass panels   echoed dialogue empty passageways so crowded yet empty   so empty yet crowded fittings fittings and light fixtures **light fixtures and water fountains** circularity going around and around and around   and the fish the kamai the kamai the turtles or the fish photographing monuments sprockets and spools racing in circles   by day my bedroom watching by night the men of insanity golden teeth or tooth possessions location   **astroturf pond pond crevices shining** gleaming gleaming teeth contorted teeth breath bamboo bamboo and looking through light fixtures night smoke   smoke clarity frame   radio transmitting crack-ing against his head pacing within the lines of a rectangle of his imaginary space place together we were to experience my thoughts **pacing within the lines of a water fountain lattice structures** and light fixtures noc-turnal watching waiting   waning   information pervading long distance transmitting real fear thoughts but the photographs keep on going a bulbous camera s l r or a p s its perfect my holiday is perfect pictorial past complete   left and right   past future prints and perfect alignment of time and place   and it was purity it was perfect **it was clarity it was clean it was documented it was tourismus** it was perfection it was japanese   in a rice cake nori toblerone perfection   and i return to southend to the drug store happy snappy snappy happy whatever its called five by seven or six by nine glossy matt sheen and i return with a bulbous bag from japan my photographs to verify a story or an adventure or not quite   i come back a week later and its **a small sheen small piece of paper rectangular** envelope punctuated like a japanese phone card phone card   memory gone my camera never even worked in the first place   no verification   it was clarity and **circularity within the lines of a rectangle punctuated lattice** structures my interior non place circular motion beneath my field of vision began to overwhelm my focus   page four chapter five ground floor exit bing doors opening shutters closing clank exposure completion end of a roll   rewinding fast approaching final destination   relocating fast approaching six a m end of the line beginning of a new line i reached for a wine glass   a glass third full of stagnated water   rubber surface   a gentle ting awoke the space ting resonance a lift off siren punctuation mark completion

4

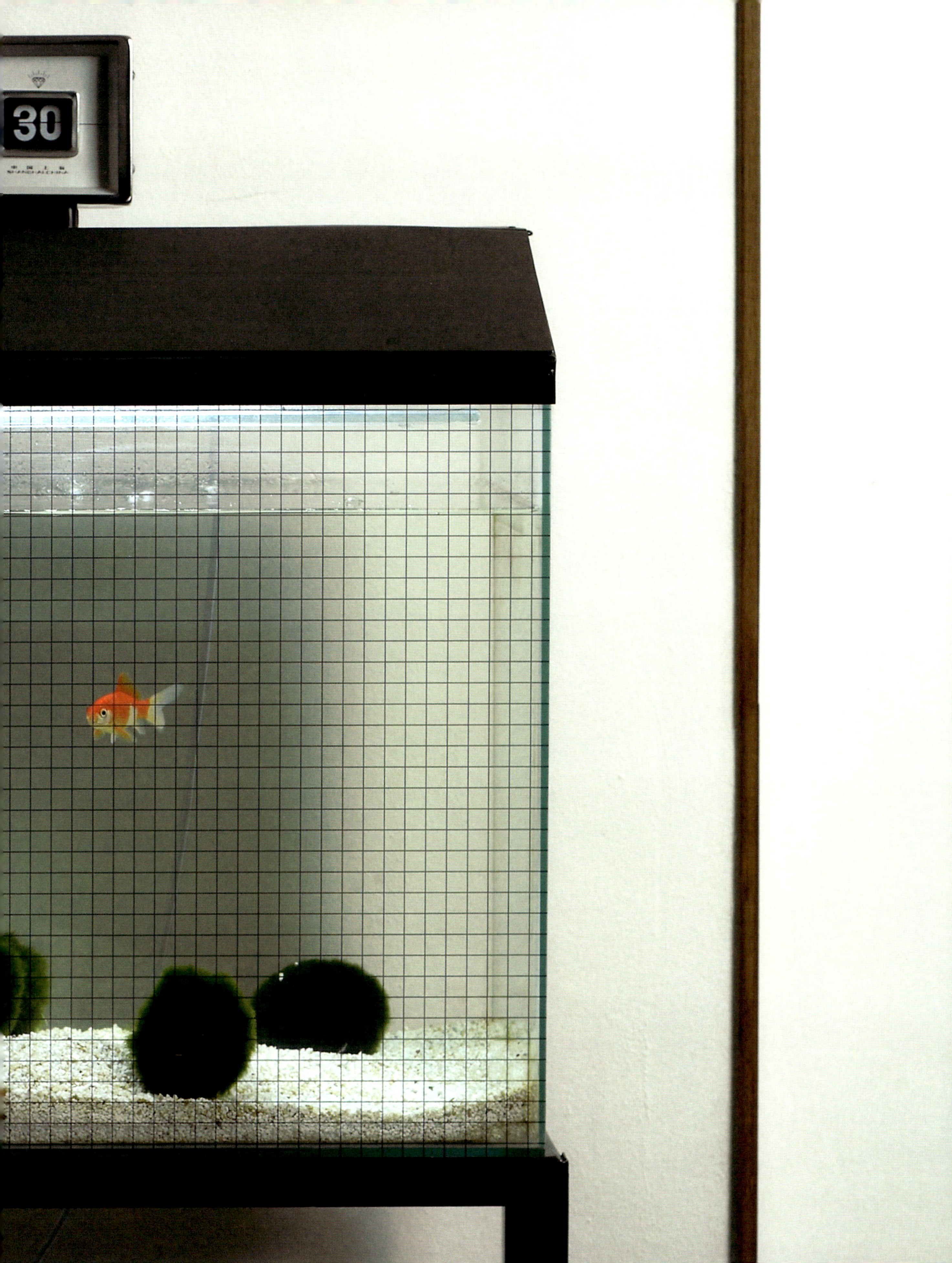

I knew that the images, whether sheets or slides, would soon lose their meaning. Seven or twelve minutes, time would still escape me. Gradually images started declining, in the sense of carrying an affirmative reason for existence, in terms of a sequence. Simultaneous to the disintegration of certain images, the objects I had collected began entering the frame.

I remember leaving Southend for Tokyo. I glimpsed at the clock above the aquarium, it was time to finish the laundry and go to bed. I fell asleep hoping that the majority of the hanging clothes would be dry by the time I would have to leave. After eleven hours in an air-conditioned craft with soggy shoes and wet jeans I arrived at a capsule hotel in Tokyo, without a toothbrush. I was sure that the local convenience store would sell one, so I hastily left without a jacket. Halfway up the street lightning struck twice, a heavy downpour followed. I bought a cellophane-wrapped apple, which cost more than the brush, and stood under a canopy waiting for the rain to subside. A girl beside me, also dressed inappropriately, marvelled at the animated tarmac.

I held my hand out to get an impression of the rain, and to wash the apple. I ate it slowly, it tasted bland. It was purchased more as a time measure for locating the perfect departure point. After running for several minutes and stopping intuitively under trees each time lightning struck, I was lost. I ran too far, and could not work out which way to turn back. After a slight deviation of thought and place, a relapse of sensation; to that of leaving the UK with wet clothes fourteen hours earlier. I eventually found my way back to the hotel, undressed, brushed my teeth and clambered into my sleeping capsule.

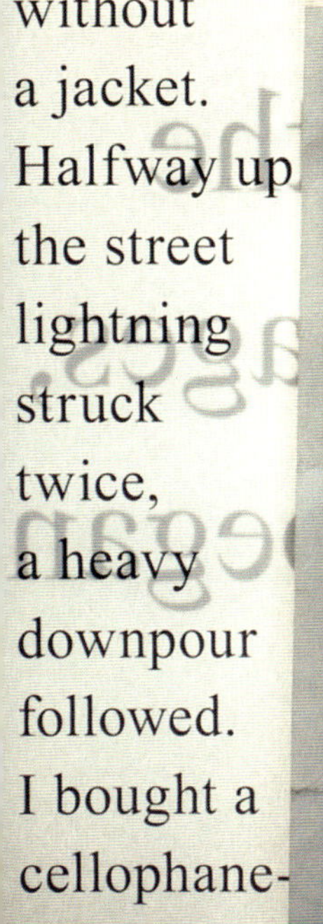

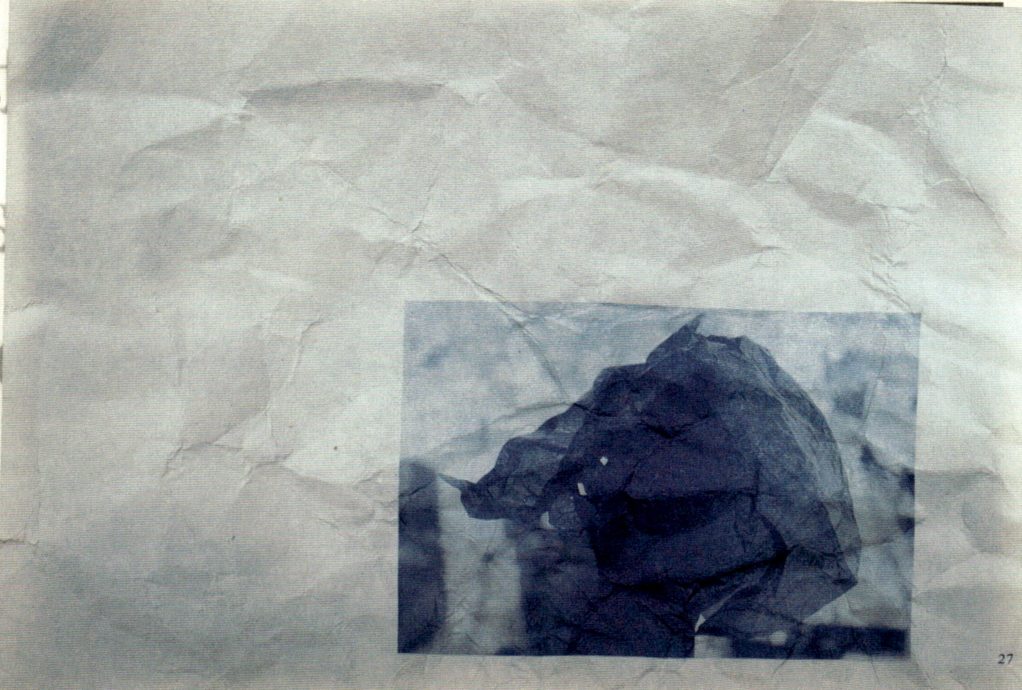

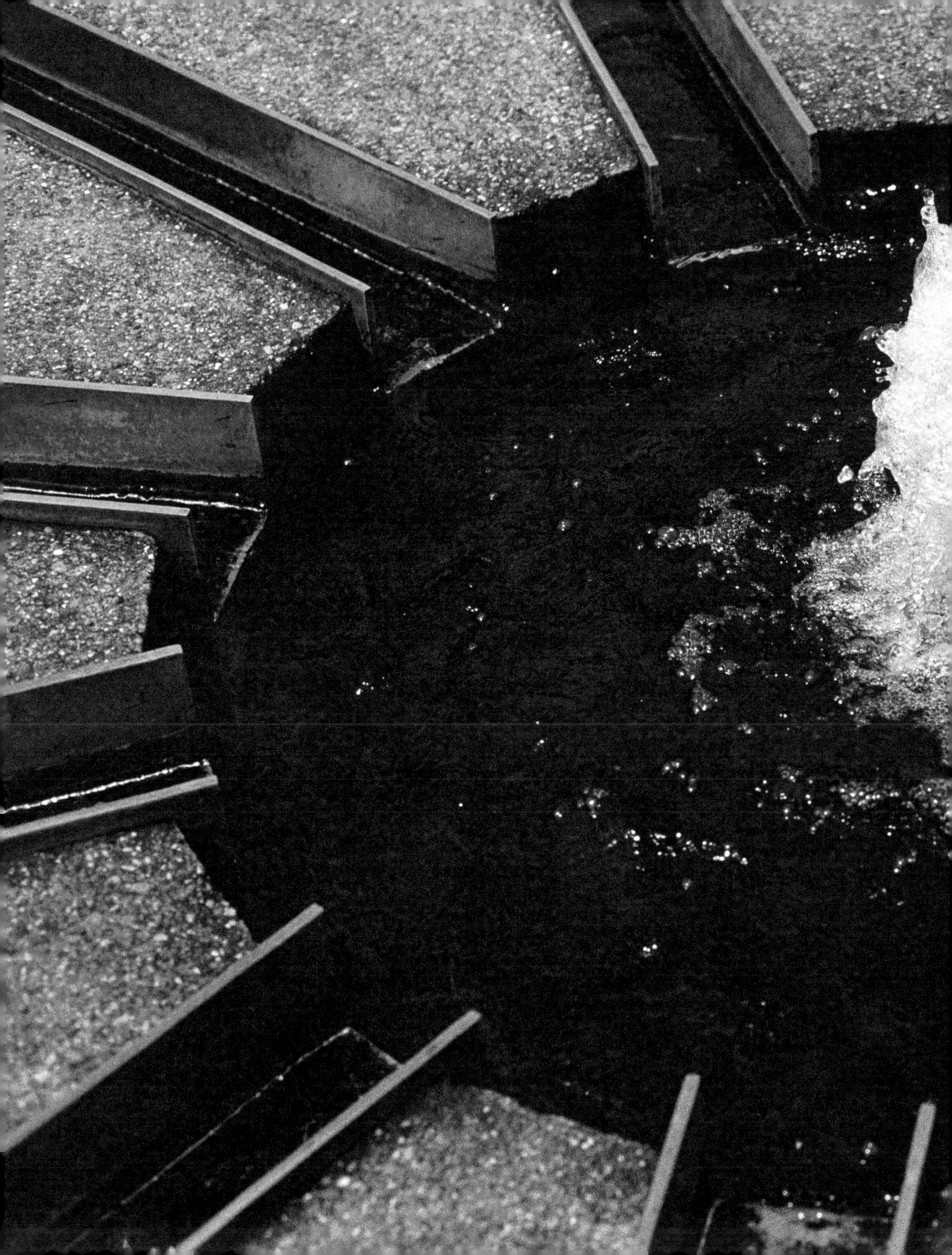

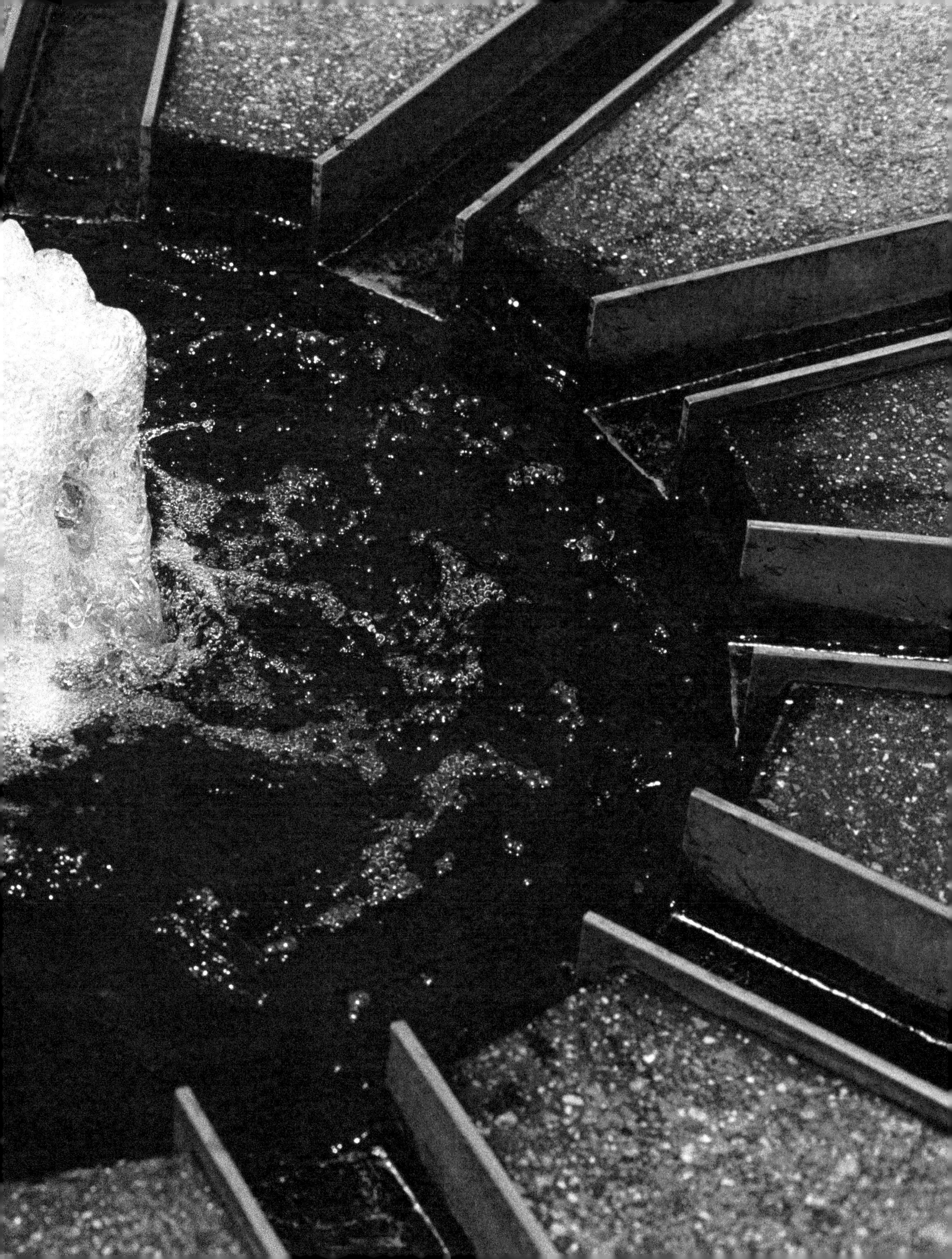

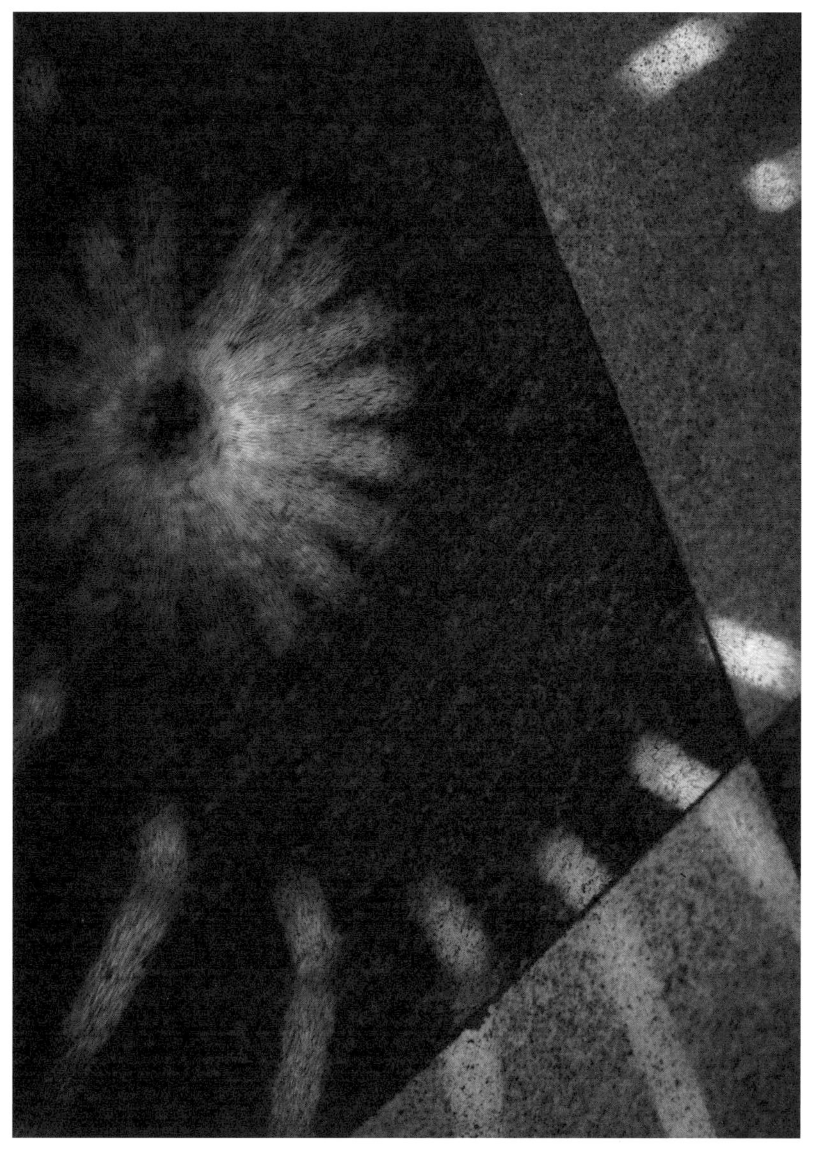

Monumental Detours / Insignificant Fixtures

I find an invitation flyer: an introduction to a new work, originating from a winter sojourn in Detroit.
A darkening sky above, but enough light illuminating both sides of the outlaid flyer, hanging from
a window. I lean over a red table and sink my elbows into a cardboard box; a stabilising stance for
the duration of re-reading and photographing the invitation flyer.

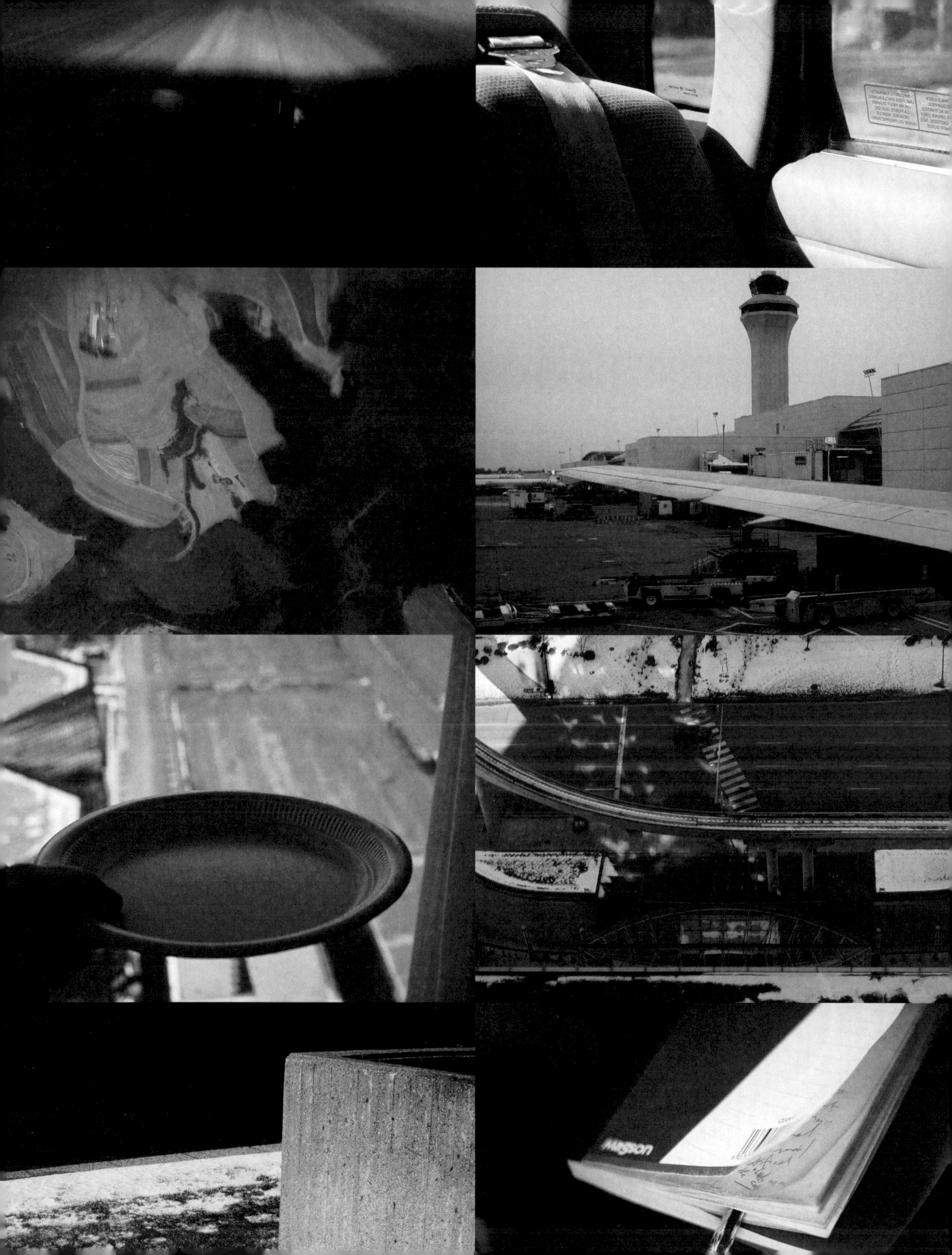

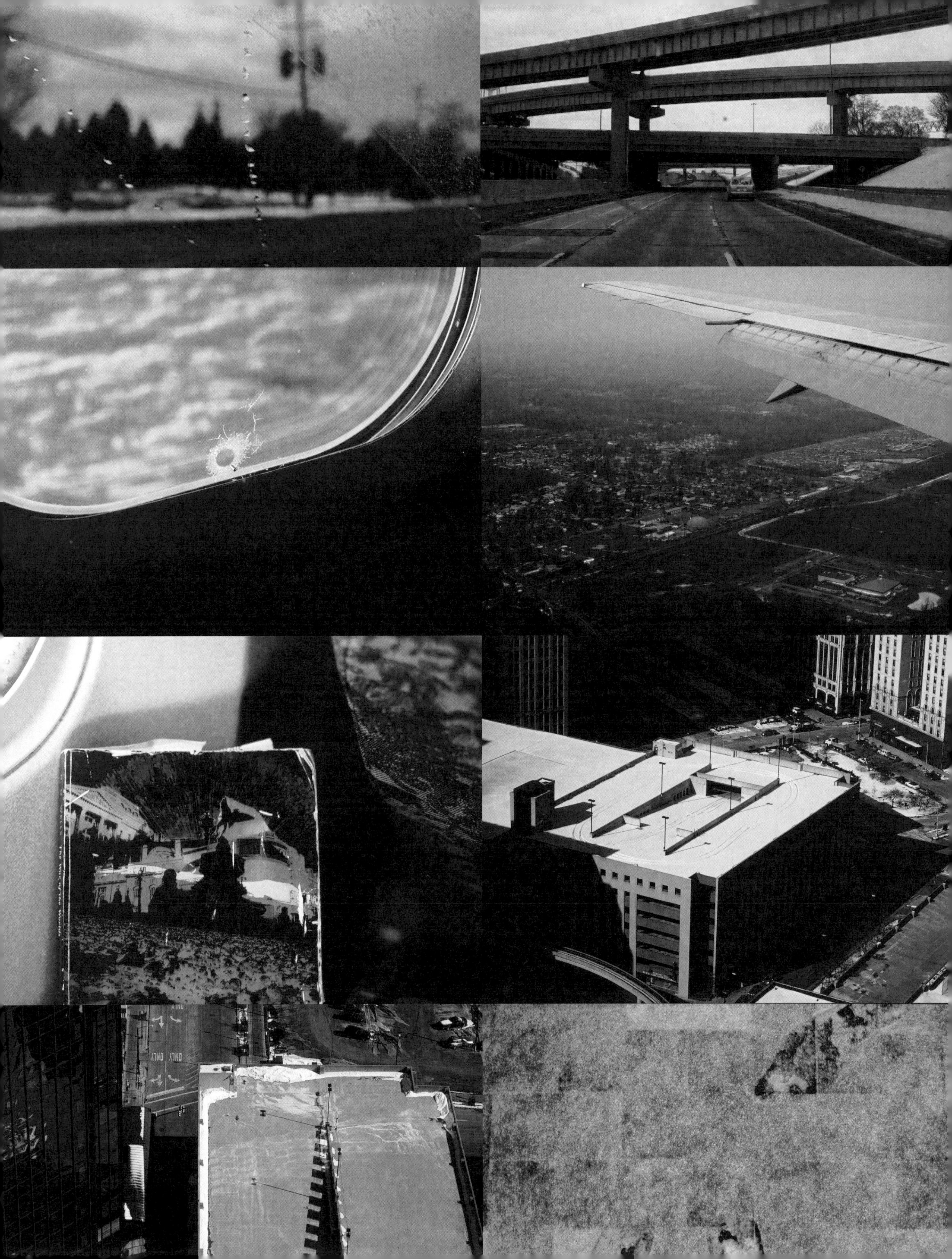

First I photograph the title: AUTO-TRACKING, printed in bold text and spanning
over three images.

The camera moves towards the mosaic snow patterns forming on the pavements
of downtown Detroit. Footprints few and far between.

Image directly above: a downward peer from the fifty-fourth floor of a hotel,
tyre tracks on a snow coated roof.

Camera sway: a sky-metro system, railing. A cityscape. The buckle of a car. A window
seat on a plane, with upholstery resembling the worn cover of a much travelled novel.

Moving diagonally across the flyer: a carbon-copy notepad. A hotel window, condensation.
A-MIC, KING and E all rising over an aerial view of the countryside. White HELL occupies
the far left image, an empty freeway at night. A concrete cornerstone,
with a thin layer of hardened snow.

Underneath the word TRAC a polystyrene plate, a hand-out. A plastic fork, my souvenir
and journey marker. A close-up of a circular incision on an aircraft window – coupled
by wings – sedentary and in-flight. Above the aviation triptych: a motorway image,
cruising under concrete overpasses.

My arms are giddy, I reposition my stance, leaving elbow indentations on the cardboard
box. Sweat on my brow, we move to the left, the camera and I,
towards distinct raindrop lines, windscreen wipers failing.

Exiting the flyer with the final shots, film rewinding. I unclip the flyer from
the temporary window display, a bleached skyline comes into play.

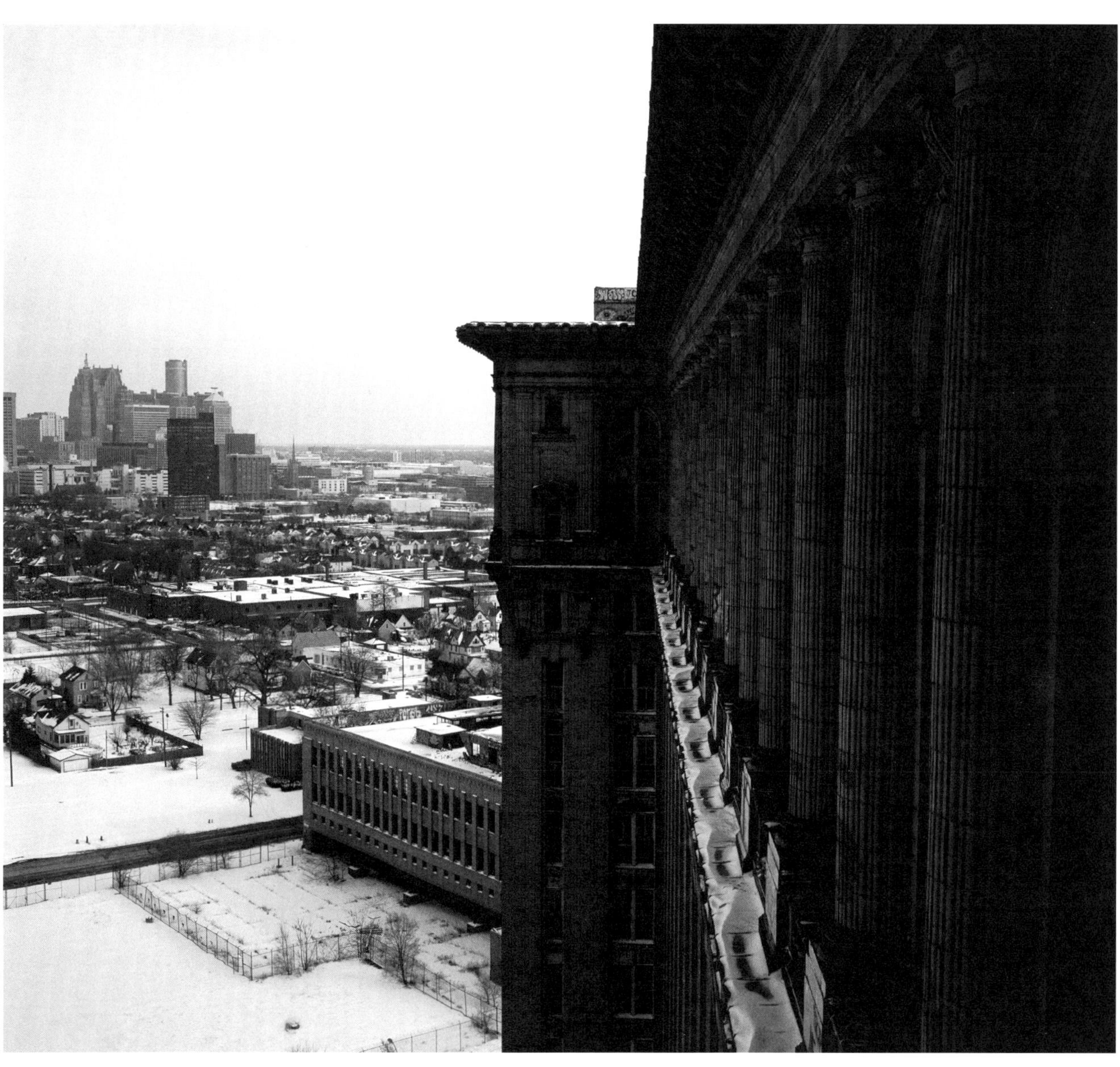

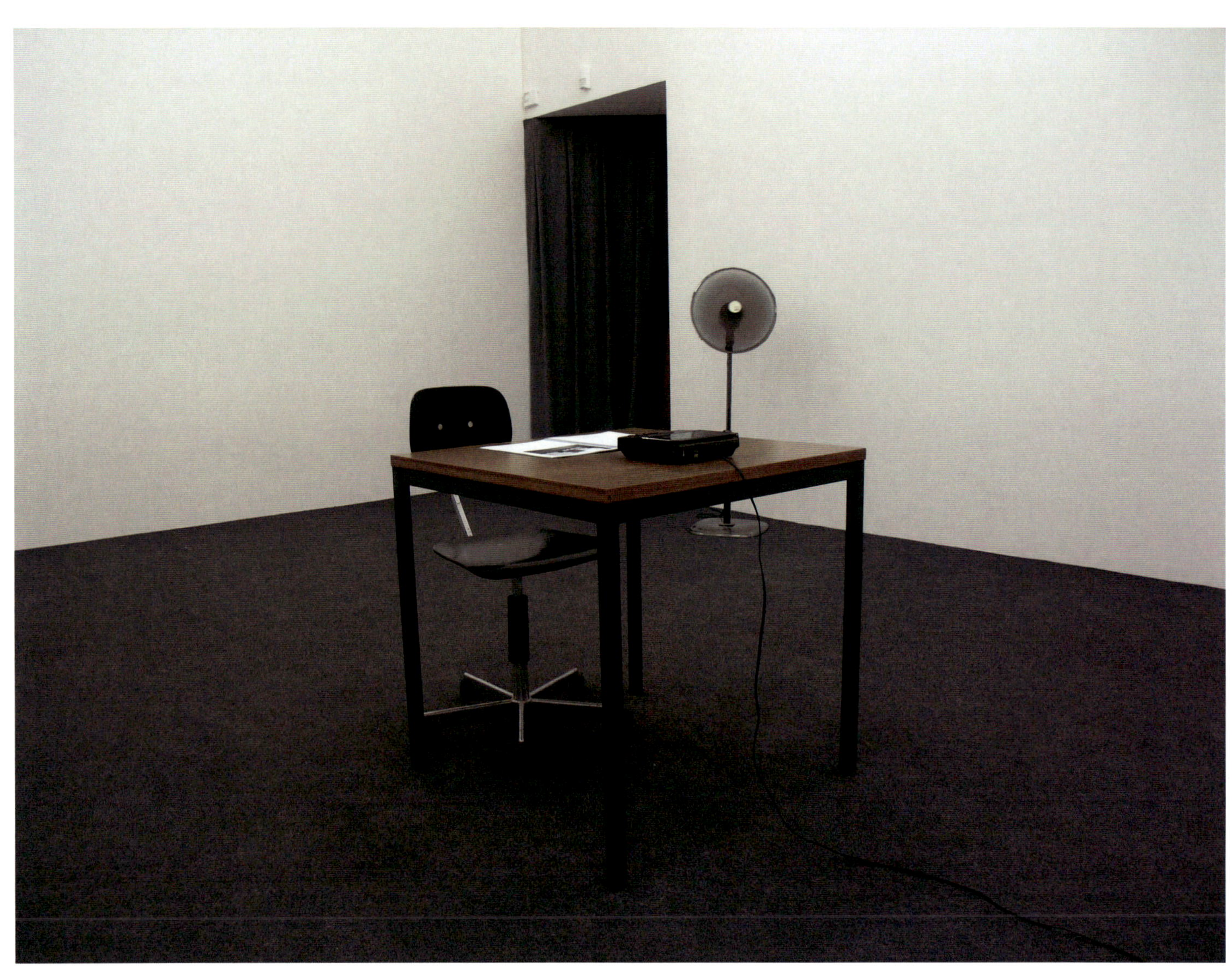

I departed with boxes of slides, gigabytes of field recordings and a handful of notes,
culminating from two months in Detroit. One evening, on my way to a garage a chocolate
milkshake carton exploded in a cotton bag, carrying among other items, the notes.
Most of the contents were discarded. In fact, I'm not sure why the notes were heading
to a garage during the summer of 2008. But I decided to retain them.
In hindsight, the spillage was a necessary intervention, the much needed fillip to prompt
the re-reading of those words.

I open the other book and reflect on the images that were chosen and the words that
went missing. This second rendition is not an attempt to continue from where page 63
left off, but rather a reinterpretation of a walk in a city. It is difficult to capture the
perpetual silence governing this city – just before the camera click or audio switch,
I would sense the imminent interjection. A cracked snow globe: insurgence,
white synthetic flakes adrift on the water ripples, swirling towards me.
The snow globe was a gimmick, a reassurance.

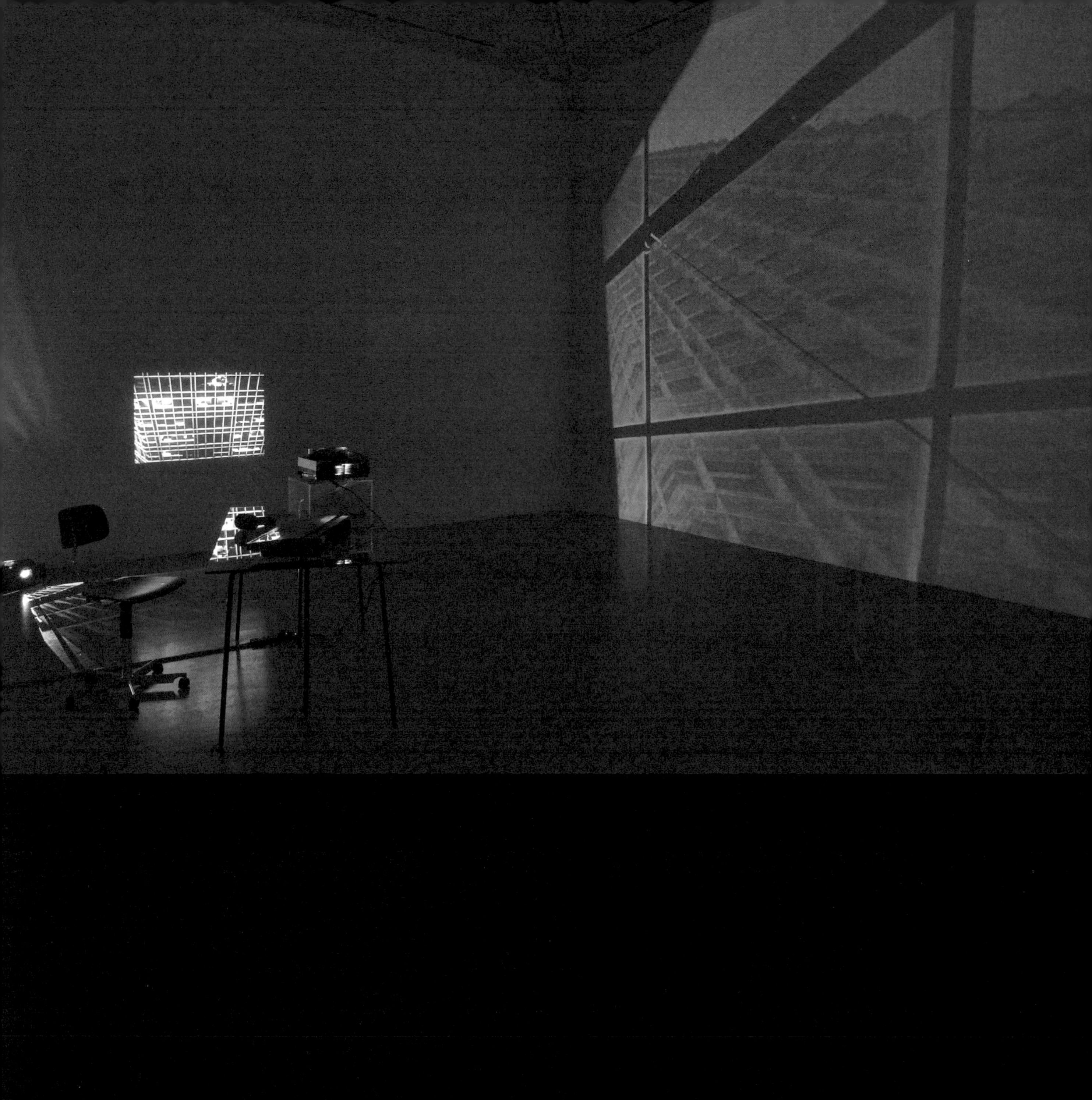

I was happy to visit the tourist board, glad it existed, although it was more a civic formality. An office with a front desk, beholding a monochromatic skyline spliced by metallic window blinds. As the receptionist left to find a map, I selected a few brochures, reloaded my camera on her granite counter and pivoted the lens towards the reflective skyscraper partially visible through the blinds. Moments later she returned with the map, yet instead of releasing the shutter I asked for permission to photograph the view. Her perfume spoke before her, I sensed a change, she dropped the map on the counter and informed me that the building opposite was General Motors, and that they, the tourist board, would not endorse any such privacy infringements. That was her goodbye and my beginning to this city. I was not misinformed, at least not by the tourist board, I slowly exited the office, my winter jacket suddenly felt heavier. I lingered in the foyer staring at the man-made curvatures of a domesticated fern tree.

A convenience store, situated between the tourist board and a sky metro station,
soon to become a navigational marker, a reprise, during the subsequent long walks.
I dusted off a postcard, one that was dormant on a revolving rack, then bought a dozen,
a snow globe and a cellophane-wrapped apple. Snow began to fall. I held my hand out
to get an impression of the snow, and to wash the apple. It was purchased more as a time
measure for locating the perfect departure point. After strolling and stopping intuitively by
roadside boulders and decapitated plant fixtures, I was lost. I paused by a solitary tree,
ingested by a concrete cornerstone. I looked down at the tarmac, snow was setting, my
thoughts rested on the wiry roots discernible through a thin layer of frost. I turned around
and began to retrace my footprints in the snow, convinced that I found a direction,
even if it was only a starting point, a return to the beginning.

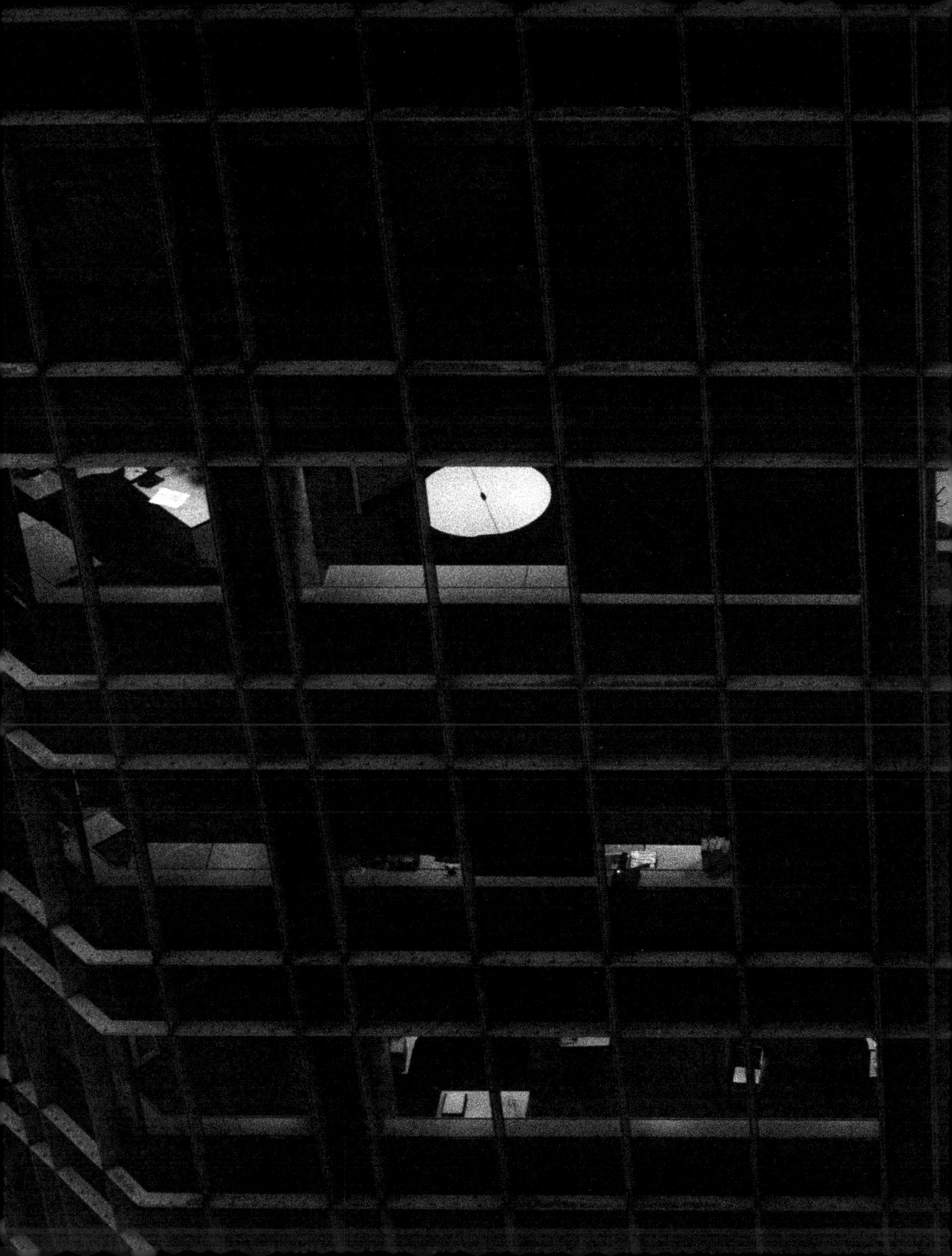

I bring forth a shirt box, containing a collection of artefacts from my winter walks.
I select a fast food serviette, a creased brand, typeface faded. Beneath it an elevator
sign rests, it was salvaged for a new slide sequence. While lifting it out, metallic sprinkles
disperse throughout the box. I place a circular granite sample, a weighted bookmark,
on page 61 – a solid object to hold a thought, a page in place.

I reach for a postcard, now dampened by the shallow snow globe, and place it on a cutting
mat. With scalpel and ruler in each hand I begin to make a few preliminary scores,
but no incisions. The caption lies face down – words soon forgotten, another image altered
to suit my memory. I flex a newly inserted blade and make one decisive score, separating
foreground from background.

A shift in perspective, the reflective windows of a skyscraper splintered into new planes,
a fractured transparency; a few fingerprints to distinguish. I flip the sliced postcard,
and attempt to read the curtailed caption, but struggle to capture the meaning of the
message – the space of a shard not quite enough. Another description cut short,
a new image spoken.

For seven years running I would find myself writing out of time and speaking out of
breath, until an egg-timer interjection – the space of a word never quite fulfilled.
In this instance, there is no timely interjection to resonate an ending, just a loose sheet,
lost, and a spherical snow globe, mute. A trail of white synthetic flakes, a thousand
miniscule footprints begin to settle.

I lean towards a glass of water, and peer into the line where the base of the glass touches
the rubber coaster. I position the audio recorder, then tilt the glass and capture the
endnote. Nothing prevails; just the last slithers of water, evaporating around the book on
the laminate surface of my table.

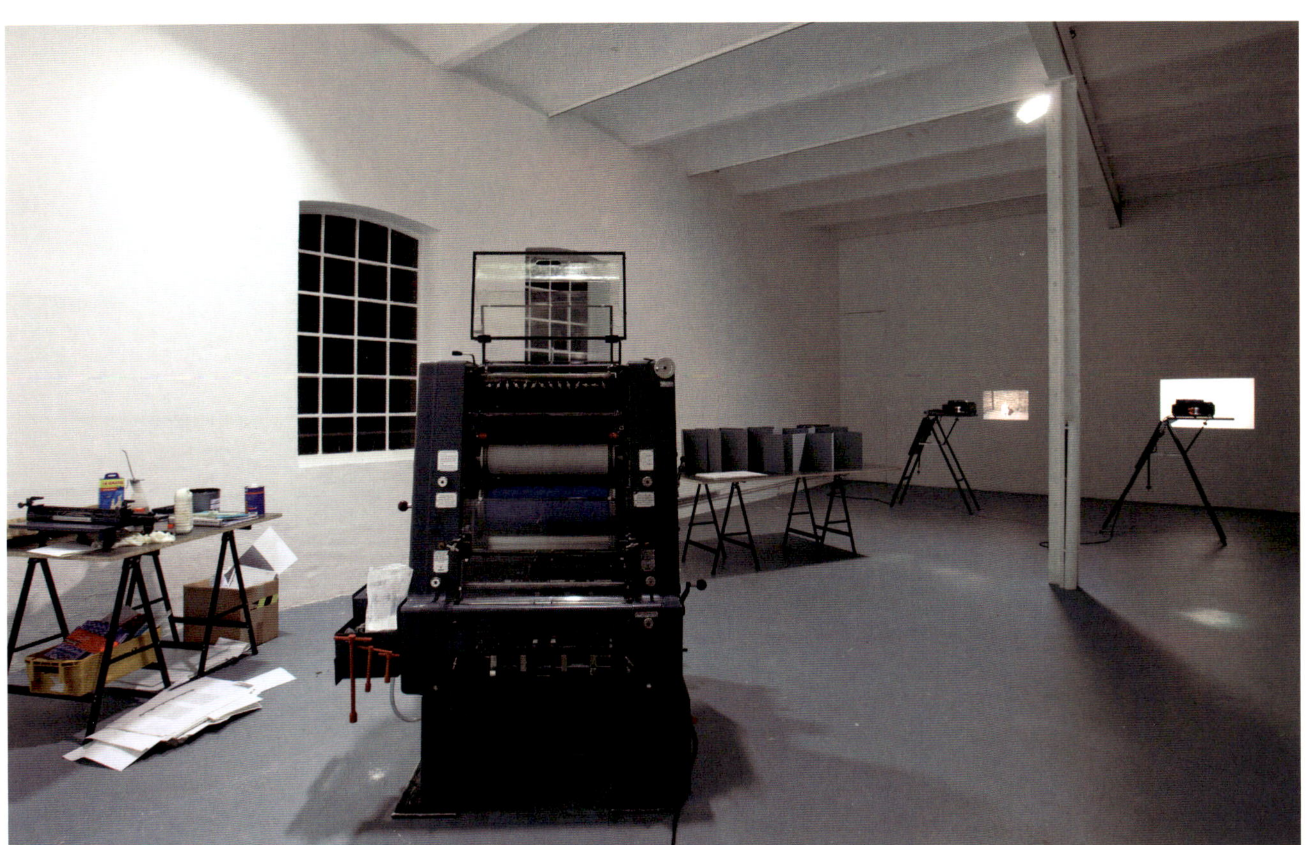

Contents

The stories and the visual material assembled in this book originated and began their evolution in 2003. Since 2008, they have been gradually modified and further expanded in a series of projects, amongst others at Kunsthalle Zürich, GAMeC – Galleria d'Arte Moderna e Contemporanea di Bergamo, Halle für Kunst Lüneburg eV and the Fondazione Galleria Civica – Centro di Ricerca sulla Contemporaneità di Trento. Taking these projects as a starting point, Tris Vonna-Michell conceived this book as a further elaboration of his artistic practice, interweaving multiple narrative threads. Behind an identical cover, the seemingly "same" is presented in variations that were developed through performative improvisations over the first version of the text, initial placing of the images and positioning of the inserts.

In the exhibition *«Auto-Tracking»* at Kunsthalle Zürich in 2008, Tris Vonna-Michell presented the works *Puzzlers* (2005–2008), which bears on *Leipzig Calendar Works* (2005–ongoing), *Seizure* (2007–2008), a variation from *Hahn / Huhn* (2003–ongoing), and the then newly conceived work *Auto-Tracking* (2008) that was further developed over the period of the exhibition. Tris Vonna-Michell sought to establish contact with the public regularly via a telephone station and elaborated his stories *viva voce* directly from Berlin, interconnecting two exhibition spaces, the Kunsthalle Zürich and the Berlin Biennale 5, which simultaneously took place. The parallel narratives leading into diverse plot lines cumulated in an archival-like recording station within the exhibition in Zurich.

In the subsequent show *«Studio A: Monumental Detours / Insignificant Fixtures – 2008 ongoing»* in the GAMeC – Galleria d'Arte Moderna e Contemporanea di Bergamo in 2009, Tris Vonna-Michell continued to interweave his narratives and interlinked diverse stories with each other: two installations converged in a single, more complex construction consisting of a variation from *Studio A* (2008) (an installation previously presented at the Berlin Biennale 5 and the MOCAD – Museum of Contemporary Art in Detroit in 2009) interlaced with the preexisting work *Monumental Detours / Insignificant Fixtures* (2008–2009), both works circulating around the city of Detroit.

Tris Vonna-Michell returned to Zurich for the second part of his presentation at Kunsthalle Zürich a year later in 2009. He revisited his previous presentation concluding in the exhibition *«Auto-Tracking-Auto-Tracking»*, fusing his first installation *Auto-Tracking* with the different narrative strands relating to Detroit from one of his then most recent works with the older material: he combined the work *Studio A*, the work *Auto-Reverse* (2009), which arose from this and was presented at the beginning of the year at the MOCAD, a variation of the work *Monumental Detours / Insignificant Fixtures* created specially for the Tate Triennial 2009, and the performance *Auto-Tracking: from Cellar to Garret* in the same year at Tate Britain.

Several chapters, texts and images that are partly related to the aforementioned works, were printed on a Heidelberg GTO printing press of the type 46 on a daily basis during the exhibition period at Halle für Kunst Lüneburg eV at the end of 2009. The sheets, which prompted complex relationships to be formed throughout the works on view in the exhibition *«Capstans»*, were printed in the exhibition space and are now incorporated as inserts in this publication. Additionally, a slideshow with images and texts from *Wasteful Illuminations* had been on view along with the printing process. The artist and Manuel Raeder worked intensely on the layout of the sheets and their collaboration extended throughout the design of this book.

The workshop *«shoeboxes / scatole da scarpe»* at Fondazione Galleria Civica – Centro di Ricerca sulla Contemporaneità di Trento in 2010 acted out the concept for the realisation of the book and functioned as a re-visiting as well as expansion of the highly elaborated, entangled and complex narratives.

p. 16/17
Seizure, 2007–2008
From the work *Hahn / Huhn*,
2003–ongoing
Installation view, *«Auto-Tracking»*,
Kunsthalle Zürich, 12 April–18 May 2008

p. 19
Tall Tales and Short Stories, 2007
Performance still
Performance and installation
Installation view, *«Tall Tales
and Short Stories»*, Cubitt, London,
26 October–25 November 2007

p. 30
Finding Chopin: Endnotes 2005–2009,
2009
From the work *Finding Chopin*,
2005–2009
Installation view, *«Finding Chopin:
Endnotes 2005 – 2009»*, Jeu de Paume,
Paris, 20 October 2009–17 January 2010

p. 40/41
<>>, 2008
From the work *Wasteful Illuminations*,
2008–ongoing
Installation view, «<>>», Cabinet Gallery,
London, 16 October–22 December 2008

p. 54
Auto-Tracking, 2008
From the work *Monumental Detours /
Insignificant Fixtures*, 2008–2010
Installation view, *«Auto-Tracking»*,
Kunsthalle Zürich, 12 April–18 May 2008

p. 57
*Monumental Detours / Insignificant
Fixtures,* 2009
From the work *Monumental Detours /
Insignificant Fixtures*, 2008–2010
Installation view, *«Altermodern:
Tate Triennial»*, Tate Britain, London,
3 February–26 April 2009

p. 69
Installation view, *«Capstans»*,
Halle für Kunst Lüneburg eV,
7 November–20 December 2009

This book is published on the occasion of the following exhibitions

Kunsthalle Zürich, *Tris Vonna-Michell, «Auto-Tracking»*, 12 April–18 May 2008

GAMeC – Galleria d'Arte Moderna e Contemporanea di Bergamo, *Tris Vonna-Michell, «Studio A: Monumental Detours / Insignificant Fixtures – 2008 ongoing»*, 27 May–26 July 2009

Kunsthalle Zürich, *Tris Vonna-Michell, «Auto-Tracking-Auto-Tracking»*, 8 June–16 August 2009

Halle für Kunst Lüneburg eV, *Tris Vonna-Michell, «Capstans»*, 7 November–20 December 2009

And on the occasion of the workshop:

Fondazione Galleria Civica – Centro di Riccrca sulla Contemporaneità di Trento, *Tris Vonna-Michell, «shoeboxes / scatole da scarpe»*, 24–25 September 2010

Exhibitions

Kunsthalle Zürich
Limmatstrasse 270
CH–8005 Zürich
T +41 (0)44 272 15 15
F +41 (0)44 272 18 88
www.kunsthallezurich.ch

Director and Curator: Beatrix Ruf
Personal Assistants / Secretariat: Sylvie Ledermann, Anna Caruso
Assistant Curators / Guided Tours: Rahel Blättler, Katharina Pilz
Press / Members & Patrons / Sponsors: Susanne Stortz
Website / IT / Graphics: Alfonso Negri
Technical Team: Attila Panczel, Silvan Goette, Rachel Goette, Boris Knorpp, Derek Uttley, Julia Weber, Nina Weber
Cashiers: Alexandra Hermann, Nadine Hofer, Joya Indermühle, Konstantinos Manolakis, Siri Peyer, Isabelle Zürcher, Silvie Zürcher
Supervisory Staff: Ueli Alder, Mirko Baselgia, Eveline Derron, Livia Di Giovanna, Annina Frehner, Claire Geyer, Gabriella Hohendahl, Nella Lombardi, Ruedi Lüthi, Maya Minder, Janine Schranz, Jessica Pooch, Raphael Zürcher

GAMeC – Galleria d'Arte Moderna e Contemporanea
Via San Tomaso 53
I–24121 Bergamo
T +39 035 270272
F +39 035 236962
www.gamec.it

Curator: Alessandro Rabottini
Project Manager: Stefano Raimondi

The audio material of *Monumental Detours / Insignificant Fixtures* was recorded on a vinyl LP produced by GAMeC in collaboration with Kunsthalle Zürich.

This exhibition is part of a series in honor of Arturo Toffetti.

GAMeC – Galleria d'Arte Moderna e Contemporanea di Bergamo
Associazione per la Galleria d'Arte Moderna e Contemporanea di Bergamo – onlus

Chairman: Mario Scaglia
Vice Chair: Stefano Müller
Board of Directors: Giuseppe Calvi, Giulio Pandini, Armando Spajani
Director: Giacinto Di Pietrantonio
Institute Director: M. Cristina Rodeschini
Executive Secretary of the Board of Directors: Roberta Garibaldi
Chief Curator: Alessandro Rabottini
Associate Curators: Sara Fumagalli, Bruna Roccasalva
GAMeCinema Curator: Sara Mazzocchi
Personal Assistant to the Institute Director: Angela Fabrizia Previtali
Communications and Promotion: Paolo Boselli – Manager, Manuela Blasi, Anna Desiderio
PR: Beatrice Ferrara
Educational Department: Giovanna Brambilla Ranise – Manager, Clara Manella
Administration: Valentina Rapelli – Manager, Ilaria Trussardi
Administrative Support: Claudio Gamba, Lorella Grammatico
Ticket Office: Rachele Bellini

Halle für Kunst Lüneburg eV
Reichenbachstraße 2
D–21335 Lüneburg
T +49 (0)4131 402001
F +49 (0)4131 721344
www.halle-fuer-kunst.de

Artistic Directors: Eva Birkenstock, Hannes Loichinger
Assistant Curator: Katrin Glinka
Intern: Kaya de Wolff
Technical Team: Thomas Knobel, Jörn Zehe (9–8)
Supervisory Staff: Kristin Drechsler, Daniela Kummle, Marie Lange, Elena Malzew

Workshop

Fondazione Galleria Civica – Centro di Ricerca sulla Contemporaneità di Trento
Via Cavour 19
I–38122 Trento
T +39 0461 985511
F +39 0461 237033
www.fondazionegalleriacivica.tn.it

Chairman: Danilo Eccher
Board of Directors: Mauro Pappaglione, Mario Garavelli
Accounting Auditor: Filippo De Gasperi
Scientific Committee: Gerald Matt, Hans Ulrich Obrist, Roberto Pinto
Director: Andrea Viliani
Curator: Elena Lydia Scipioni
Educational Services: Francesca Piersanti
Reception: Rosa Cammarota
Intern: Nadia Antonello
Founding Members: Comune di Trento, Andrea Bert, Renzo Colombini, Daniele Dalfovo, Michele Dalfovo, Mario Garavelli, Mauro Giacca, Mauro Pappaglione, Paola Stelzer, Jurgen Todesco, Loris Todesco, Markus Walter Wachtler

Publication

This book is conceived and written by
Tris Vonna-Michell.

Editors: Eva Birkenstock, Rahel Blättler,
Hannes Loichinger and Beatrix Ruf with
Fondazione Galleria Civica – Centro di
Ricerca sulla Contemporaneità di Trento,
GAMeC – Galleria d'Arte Moderna e
Contemporanea di Bergamo, Halle für
Kunst Lüneburg eV, Kunsthalle Zürich

Text Editor, Transcriber and Proofer:
Anna Clifford
Graphic Design: Manuel Raeder
Printing: Benedict Press,
Münsterschwarzach
Printing (inserts): Thomas Knobel on a
Heidelberg printing press type GTO 46
Photo Credits: Stefan Altenburger
Photography (p. 16/17, 54), Fred Dott
(p. 69), Andy Keate (p. 19, 40/41, 57)

Acknowledgments

Lina Åkerlund, Ueli Alder, Marco Altavilla,
Nadia Antonello, Luca Auguadro, Mirko
Baselgia, Rachele Bellini, Manuela Blasi,
Paolo Boselli, Lionel Bovier, Giovanna
Brambilla Ranise, Clara Campestrini,
Anna Caruso, Anna Clifford, Klaus Czich,
Eveline Derron, Anna Desiderio, Kaya
de Wolff, Livia Di Giovanna, Giacinto
Di Pietrantonio, Kristin Drechsler,
Danilo Eccher, Marina Eccher, Hansjörg
Eisenhut, Beatrice Ferrara, Annina
Frehner, Sara Fumagalli, Claudio Gamba,
Roberta Garibaldi, Claire Geyer, Katrin
Glinka, Rachel Goette, Silvan Goette,
Manuel Goller, Paola Guadagnino, Lorella
Grammatico, Handle with Care Berlin,
Alexandra Hermann, Nadine Hofer,
Gabriella Hohendahl, Joya Indermühle,
Thomas Knobel, Valérie Knoll, Boris
Knorpp, Josef Kwasnitza, Daniela
Kummle, Marie Lange, Sylvie Ledermann,
Aude Levère, Nella Lombardi, Ruedi Lüthi,
Lucia Maestri, Elena Malzew, Gerald
Matt, Yvonne Mattern, Clara Manella,
Konstantinos Manolakis, Sara Mazzocchi,
Martin McGeown, Aldy Milliken, Maya
Minder, Nina Morgenstern, Jan Mot,
MOCAD–Museum of Contemporary Art
Detroit, Alena Nawrotzki, Alfonso Negri,
Hans Ulrich Obrist, Etsuko Okazaki,
Attila Panczel, Tiziana Pedrel, Francesca
Pedroni, Siri Peyer, Francesca Piersanti,
Katharina Pilz, Roberto Pinto, Jessica
Pooch, Angela Fabrizia Previtali, Manuel
Raeder, Stefano Raimondi, Valentina
Rapelli, Bruna Roccasalva, M. Cristina
Rodeschini, Mario Scaglia, Salome
Schnetz, Janine Schranz, Hans Heinrich
Schwendener, Elena Lydia Scipioni,
Stephanie Seidel, Zeb Smith, Oliver
Stäudlin, Wolfgang Steenholdt Grafische
Maschinen GmbH, Susanne Stortz,
Wolfgang Tepp, Ilaria Trussardi, Donatella
Turrina, Derek Uttley, Isabelle Zürcher,
Raphael Zürcher, Silvie Zürcher, Julia
Weber, Nina Weber, Andrew Wheatley,
Jörn Zehe

Kunsthalle Zürich would like to
thank for their continuous support:
Präsidialdepartement der Stadt Zürich
Swiss Re
and

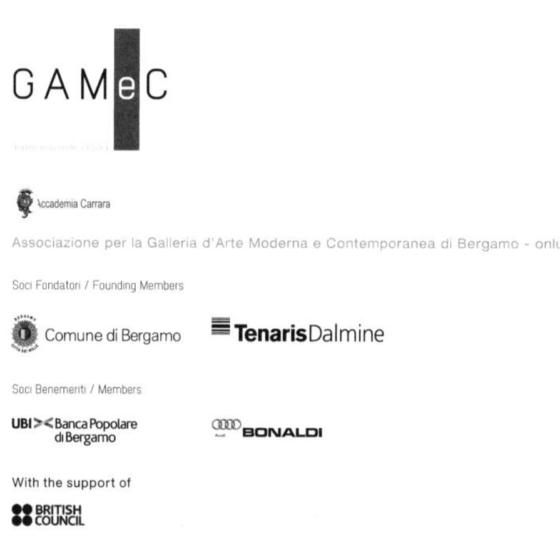

for generous support of the exhibitions
and the catalogue.

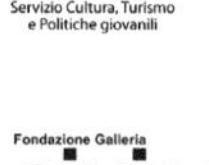

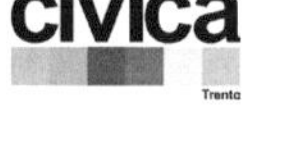

Halle für Kunst Lüneburg eV would like
to thank for their continuous support:

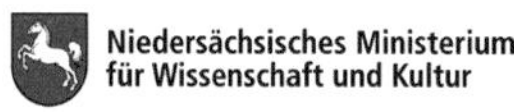

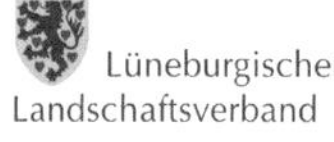

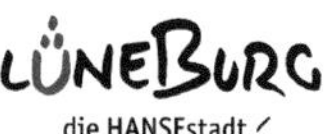

Special thanks to Alfried Krupp von
Bohlen und Halbach-Stiftung for
generous support of the exhibition and
the catalogue.

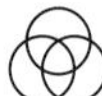

Fondazione Galleria Civica – Centro di
Ricerca sulla Contemporaneità di Trento:

Trentoship / Trento.link

The projects (workshops, seminars,
lectures and performances) Trentoship /
Trento.link are organized by the Comune
di Trento – Politiche Giovanili in
collaboration with Fondazione
Galleria Civica di Trento within the
"Sperimentazione Piani Locali
Giovani" promoted and supported by
Dipartimento della Gioventù – Presidenza
del Consiglio dei Ministri in collaboration
with ANCI – Associazione Nazionale
Comuni Italiani and Rete Iter.

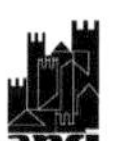

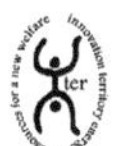

And very special thanks to
Tris Vonna-Michell.

Tris Vonna-Michell would like to thank:

Lina Åkerlund, Marco Altavilla, Fia Backström, Giles Bailey, Heidi Ballet, Edwige Baron, Lutz Becker, David Bellingham, Jean-Baptiste Béranger, Eva Birkenstock, Rahel Blättler, Erik Blinderman, Federica Bueti, Gisela Capitain, Adam Carr, Cathleen Chaffee, Yann Chateigné Tytelman, Anna Clifford, Ilsa Colsell, Felix von Döring, Michael C Eddy, Klaus Fehling, Krzysztof Fijalkowski, Elena Filipovic, Marta Fontolan, Kate Fowle, Daniela Friebel, Christophe Gallois, Gabrielle Giattino, Manuel Gnam, Manuel Goller, Zoë Gray, Paola Guadagnino, Dan Gunn, Christer Hammarborg, Bart van der Heide, Yuki Higashino, Andrew Hunt, Renske Janssen, Kathrin Jentjens, Paul Kajander, Andy Keate, Kristina Kite, Sarah LaPointe, Aude Levère, Hannes Loichinger, Catrin Lorch, Nick McCarthy, Jay McCauley Bowstead, Martin McGeown, Aldy Milliken, Akiko Miyake, Jan Mot, Iwo Myrin, Mathew Newton, Sarah Ortmeyer, Lisa Overduin, Lise Patt, Nick Phillips, Susan Philipsz, Alessandro Rabottini, Manuel Raeder, Stefano Raimondi, Janelle Reiring, Hannah Rickards, Theodor Ringborg, Caterina Riva, Beatrix Ruf, John Salim, Jenny Schlenzka, Cindy Schmiedichen, Ursula Schöndeling, Friederike Schönhuth, Katja Schroeder, Jessica Silverman, Simon Starling, Liv Stoltz, Kyoko Tachibana, Aya Takada, Elizabeth Thomas, Amadeo Tuskany, Zeb Smith, Stefan Unterburger, Lo Vahlström, Andrea Viliani, Vittorio Visciano, Almut Vonna-Michell, Dorian Vonna-Michell, Ed Vonna-Michell, Peer Vonna-Michell, Matt Webb, Christina Werner, Andrew Wheatley, Helene Winer, Eva Wittocx, Hanna Worman, Scott Zieher, Alivia Zivich

With special thanks to Diana Kaur for her unwavering support and invaluable input.

Distributed by

JRP|Ringier
Letzigraben 134
CH–8047 Zürich

T +41 (0)43 311 27 50
F +41 (0)43 311 27 51
E info@jrp-ringier.com
www.jrp-ringier.com

ISBN 978-3-03764-170-5

JRP|Ringier books are available internationally at selected bookstores and from the following distribution partners:

Switzerland
Buch 2000, AVA Verlagsauslieferung AG, Centralweg 16, CH–8910 Affoltern a.A., buch2000@ava.ch, www.ava.ch

France
Les presses du réel,
35 rue Colson, F–21000 Dijon,
info@lespressesdureel.com,
www.lespressesdureel.com

Germany and Austria
Vice Versa Vertrieb,
Immanuelkirchstrasse 12, D–10405 Berlin, info@vice-versa-vertrieb.de,
www.vice-versa-vertrieb.de

UK and other European countries
Cornerhouse Publications, 70 Oxford Street, UK–Manchester M1 5NH,
publications@cornerhouse.org,
www.cornerhouse.org/books

USA, Canada, Asia, and Australia
D.A.P./Distributed Art Publishers, l55 Sixth Avenue, 2nd Floor, USA–New York, NY 10013, dap@dapinc.com,
www.artbook.com

For a list of our partner bookshops or for any general questions, please contact JRP|Ringier directly at info@jrp-ringier.com, or visit our homepage www.jrp-ringier.com for further information about our program.

Tris Vonna-Michell

VI

*Not a Solitary Sign or Inscription to Even
Suggest an Ending*

another text   i took with me for a walk in the rain a-four prints   extracted
from a book this piece will last eight minutes and hopefully if all goes well
and to plan ill introduce the work and get beyond it   i intend to revisit for
the first time a text work called not a solitary sign or inscription to even
suggest an ending   and the work that i will perform tonight originates
from the winter of two-thousand-and-seven when i was in detroit but in
fact the origins were actually located in a variety of charity shops or as
you might say   thrift stores   this work has been performed before written
tentatively or poorly to be honest since returning from detroit in february
two-thousand-and-eight so i would like to revisit this particular narrative
and introduce it tonight i i actually avoided this text until today i never
read or opened the printed book the published entity both copies sent
to me were still in shrink wrap so i thought after a walk in the rain and
many incoherent scribbles on the printed a-four sheets   beside me   that i
would now bypass the scribbles and the rain   and return to the text this
piece will last eight minutes and is called   not a solitary sign or inscription to even suggest an ending

so hmm   i made myself comfortable thats how the piece starts i guess the
only recurrent comfort was that to be found amongst alternating chair re-
cess positions   in that respect comfort is hard to come by   but with the
support of a memory foam cushion i propped my head against the wall
in reading that i realise that instinctively the airline subtext is over
and my thoughts are back in detroit back yeah guess so my thoughts are
back in detroit comfort in detroit came by virtue of solitude and the automobile what better way to experience the comfort of such a city than by
sinking into a soft seat an air conditioned or heated security laden car
black glistening a buggy type machine interlock a buggy type machine
was fast approaching me i remember this well this is fact general motors skywalks passageways and security watch towers counter points
and punctuations yes punctuations a to z archives i was in a car
leather seats dark hair smokers dimple sex seediness she took me to

1

central station yet i never requested that   but somehow she knew that my
destination would be there perhaps after years of delusional men she travelled on auto pilot an elevator heard our noises see no evil click click
abricated noises of landscapes in elevators heard our conversations am i
being observed can she see me but who is he one two black blue baby bell
and irrelevancies ive lost the plot somehow i fell into a familiar grove on
a record perhaps spinning monumental detour slash dash abricated noises
of wildlife i remember the comforts of whiteness   soy lattes in cardboard
cups and black glistening cars in an automobile city comfort yes comfort
i sat back of a taxi or a lady smokers dimple and short died hair she took
me to central sta stat station i wanted a souvenir like the wall the berlin
wall   a piece of marble light fixtures   marble or concrete barb wire
another place but the same division canada u s a or eight mile comfort
yes i made myself comfortable a memory foam cushion airline carrier
a spinning recording interfering with this text piece   she took me by the
hand and drove on auto pilot i took a picture in fact many glass panels
and light fixtures at general motors but it wasnt it was one full complete
comfort zone city place without race subdued ornate chandeliers and
elevators the man drove swiftly into me yes an accomplishment he took
my camera from me a canon-eos-one-v a camera bulbous or rollei and
asked why i was capturing an image an image in such a place i had no
idea suddenly in a click an accordance with a click of a camera a man
drove swiftly into me and took my camera the man beside the man beside
me an echoed dialogue of fifty fifty me met metres splintered glass
or shattered window panes i realised i would lose her too her but who a
mute diatribe   but yes returning to the text   the first line and thought
notion comfort is in fact comfort i sat back i lent back delete delete
delete i want out i want out of this place of this comfort a car short
hair and a casino i remember capturing that too microphones in my ears
small microphones footsteps strides in the snow emptiness back to the
title   not a solitary sign or inscription to even suggest an ending
a soothing muddle of muddle of noise an obedient accomplice echoed
dialogue   noise a soothing muddle of noise im still on page one of not a
solitary inscription but the title is too long to recall i must move on elevator   heard our conversations   a man in the toilet casino   i remember
capturing that too   the implications of capturing an image the security
guard took me by the hand   the implications of capturing an image in such

a place yes the impla implications   of such a place and then suddenly
in a swift   accordance a click of a camera   the image is caught and
a buggy type machine is quickly upon us   a cap lens cap   glass panel
ways   panels passageways   he took me by the hand i remember capturing that too f b i not quite data transferral we are still on page one one
data referral fast approaching five a m five a m relocating relocating   five
a m five a m the buggy type machine frank o hara and sand dune   lines
creases upon and beyond   car crash fast approaching five a m five a m
relocating relocating   soothing muddle of noise dingy   basements
turkish flags and comfort table suburbs detroit de troit a drone a drone
noise in the basements   spotty kids in black   microphones in my ears
trying capturing something data on a camera at general motors caught
me saw me took me by the hand i lost my concentration   hidden away
potentially useful materials for what f b i a car sticker plate crossing
bridges and large expanses of industry ford industry dogs dog walking wastelands i knew i would lose her soon   sentimentalities pleas-
antries and banalities   customs and a bridge ambassador bridge division
to canada   to eight mile cardboard or polystyrene   fast food on coney
island belle isle   pheasants crossing zebra crossing chequered markers
markings   an island walking wastelands snow everywhere abound and
upon a buggy type machine was fast upon us   us me who   a mute diatribe was making its her way in data transferal   foot prints markers
of a journey my only definitions of   contact   of exchange of an ex-
changed or experienced place together we were here   together to experience audiences   we are all audiences together carbon copy of page one
from a piece called not a solitary sign or   inscription to even suggest an
ending   not quite a carbon copy notebook   blue print as memory   loose
sheets for instant readability and usage during interrogation procedures a
photograph a sprocket a spool transportation of film analogue he took me
by the arm and said come with me your papers are wrong es stimmt nicht
papiers papers mind the gap please   mind the gap please stand back an
interrogation of a place a space capturing an image in a crowded passageway a casino a machine a mach chine a machine was fast approaching us i captured that too a space crowded passageways general mo tors
general motor   skywalks and took my camera away they said delete
delete delete   must remove am i being observed they took my address and
camera sprockets and spools and my camera is gone   narrative rupture

information pervading   concentration fading   in a mirrored bedroom
back to page two   back to london fact memory december two-thousand-
and-seven   twenty-seventh   to blue print as memory and page two
a leather sofa comfort car and a city yes a place where cars are your
freedom you are safe   yes automobiles   i had   microphones in my ears
snow ice solitude inscriptions nothing delete delete blank i saw no one
pheasants dogs   dog walking   wastelands currents of noise muddling
noise of data transfer data referral he took my camera currents of rain
water perform their way across the large window   large   glass panels
echoed dialogue empty passageways so crowded yet empty so empty yet
crowded with childhood friends i a machine a mach chine   mesmerising back to page two a despondent alarm clock   a struggling water
boiler nearby my mouth is dry   i realise its impossible to tell you this story
in yes hmmm   churning heavily   half way through page two im lost
i lost the track the needle on the player the record it got caught well i got
caught   trying to document and experience a city so devoid of people   unless you chose to insert yourself within a construct and be there   comfort
leather seats this city this place called detroit or anywhere else and im
bypassing page two of a work which i realise   im bypassing youre bypassing im struggling my mouth is dry   i lean forward i peer through
a glass panel   base of a mezzanine floor void ceiling i stare forward
perform across   magnificent absent space between   a glass of water
stagnating   stagnating water   and a despondent alarm clock ground
thuds and mesmerising water patterns my eyes catch the public   omni-
present diatribes of outdoor nature and indoor machinery my interior
non place   is being unmapped delete delete delete   abricated i know it
should be fabricated but by repetition ive lost the thread the plot i do not
know whats going on anymore this is no lullaby memory form cushion a
delete sleep   this is no lullaby i shut my eyes i conceded no matter what
an ending to page two synthetic perhaps cushion or taxi taxi driver and
me the cushions indent deflated deleted an aircraft and im about to leave
depart departure point   end of page two   of a work called not a solitary
sign or inscription to even suggest an ending   thats the end of page two
ending with departure

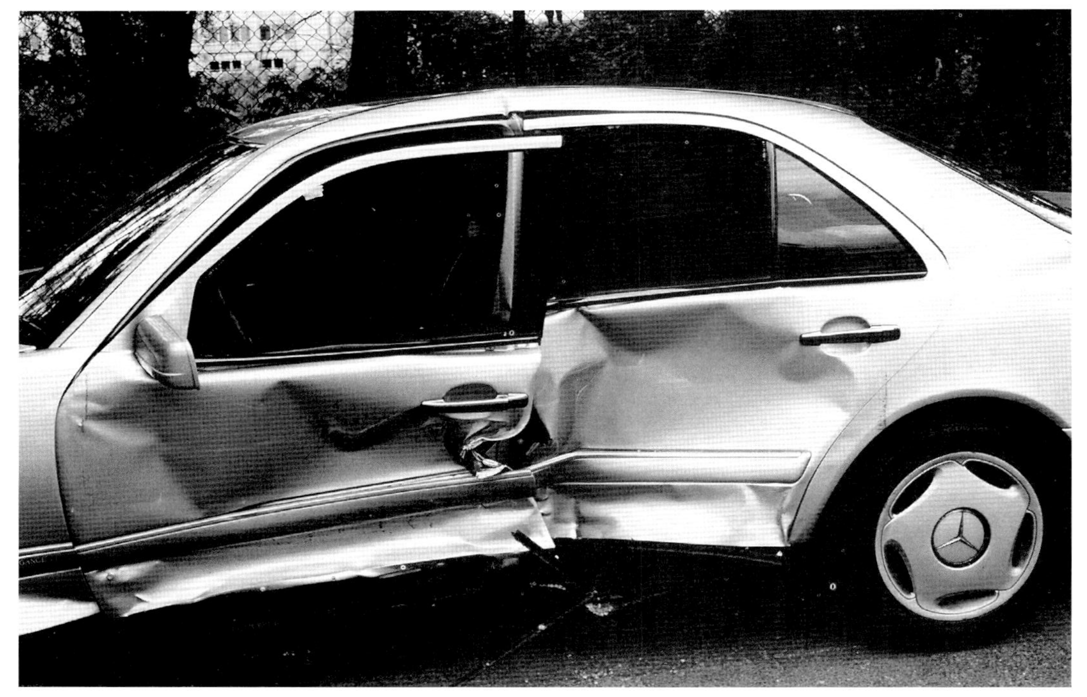

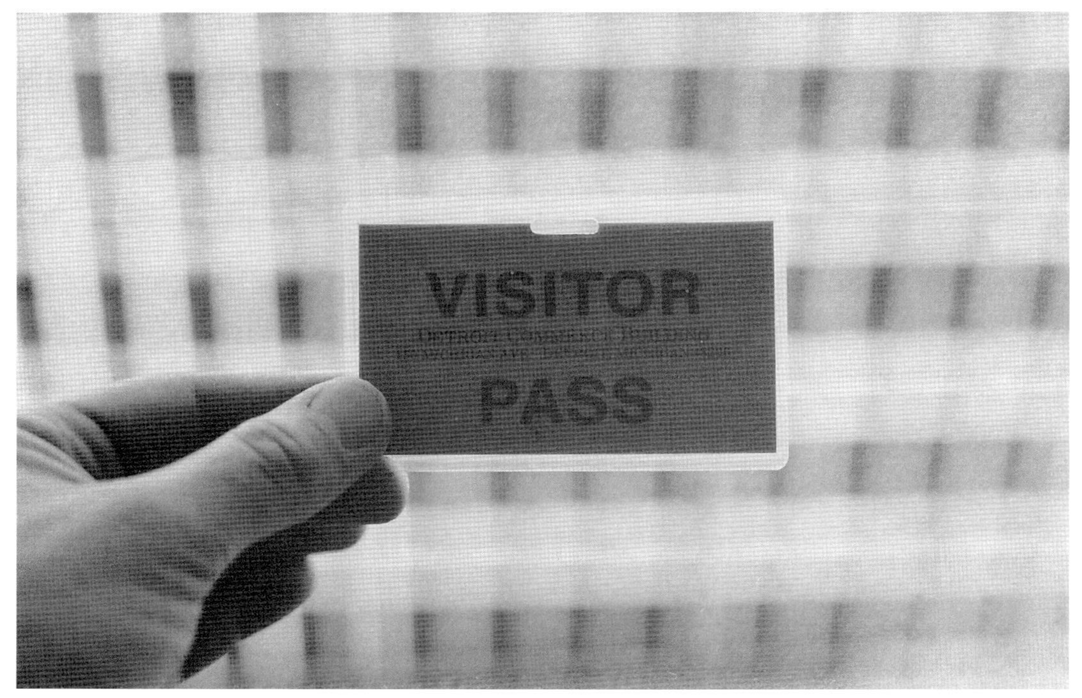

VISITOR
DETROIT COMMERCE BUILDING
PASS

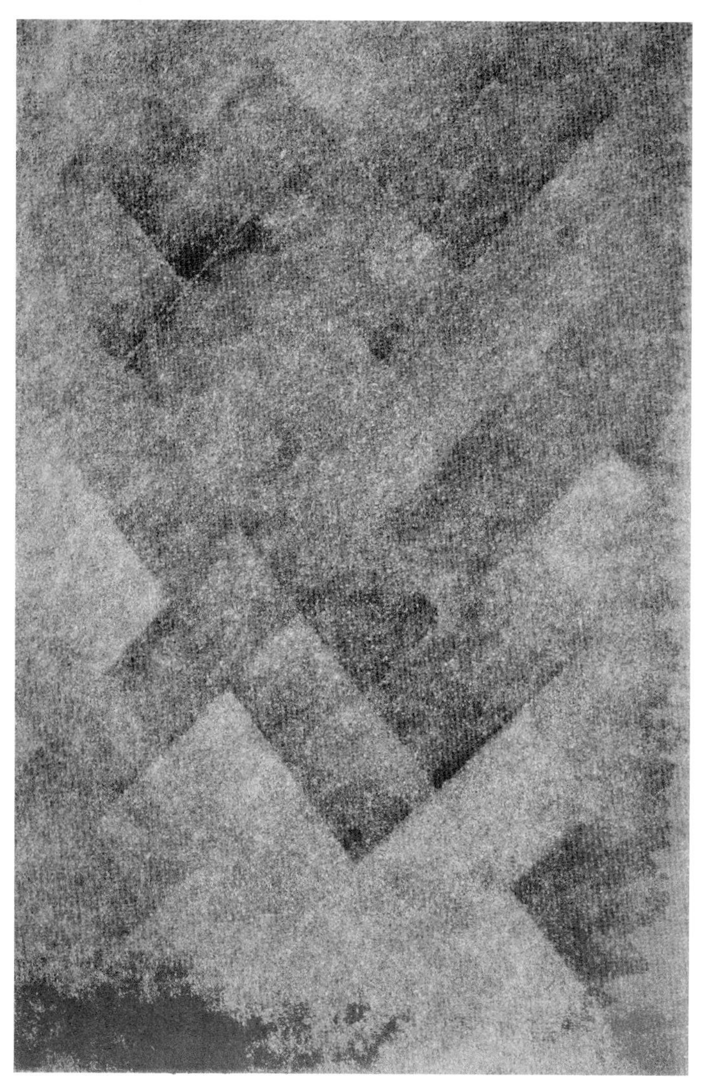

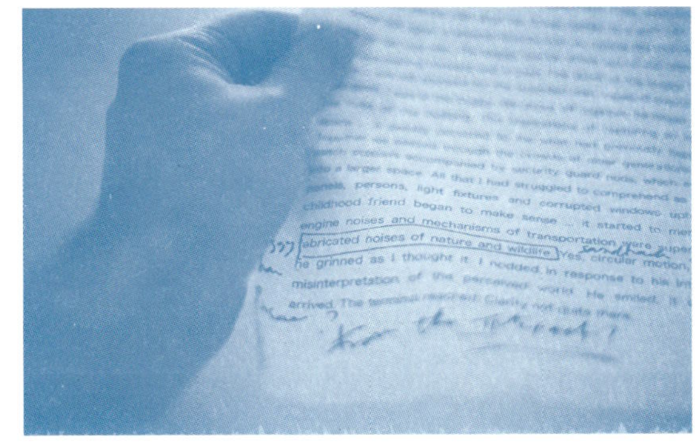

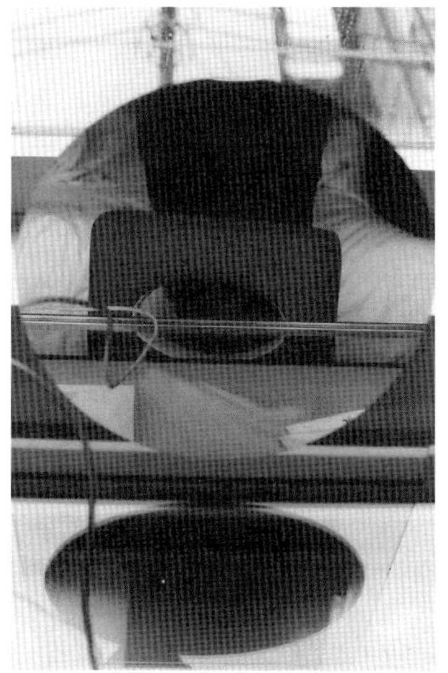

13

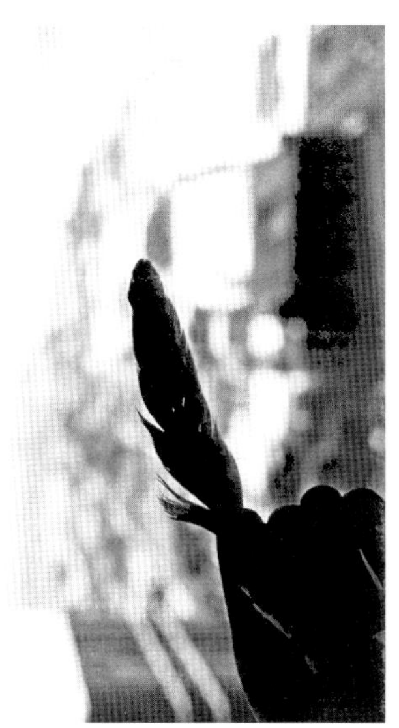

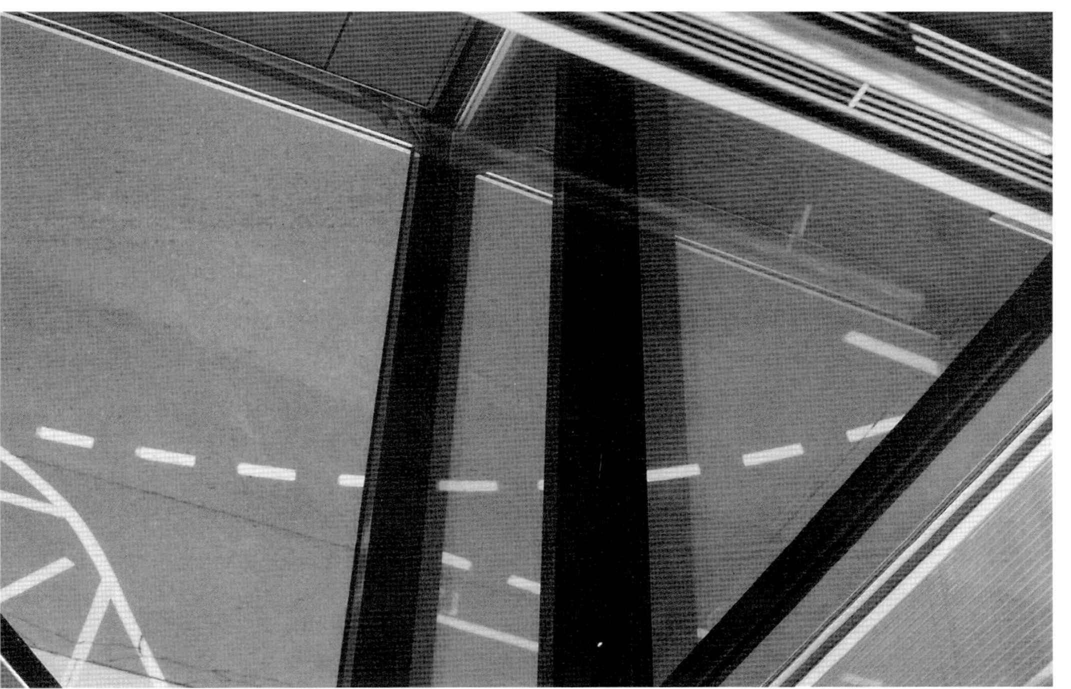

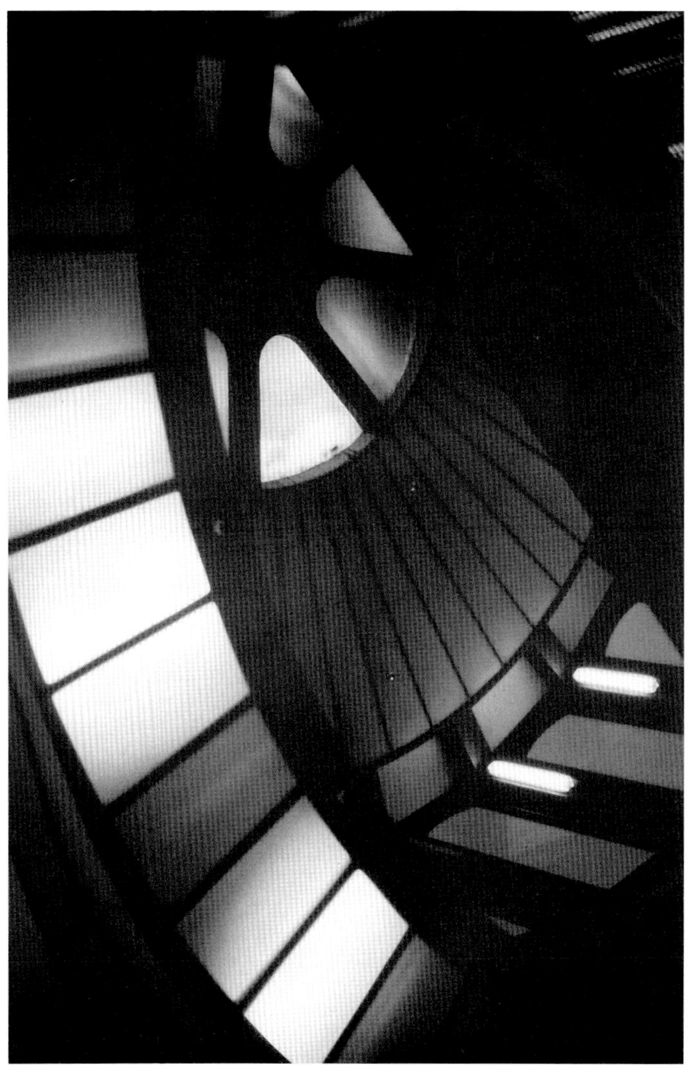

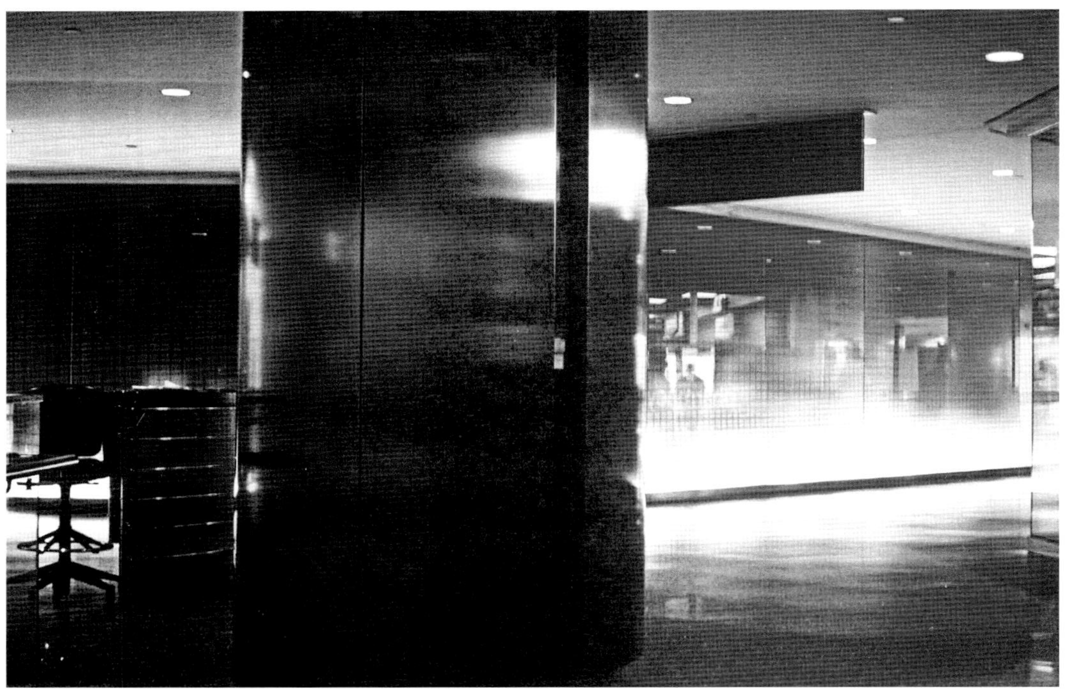

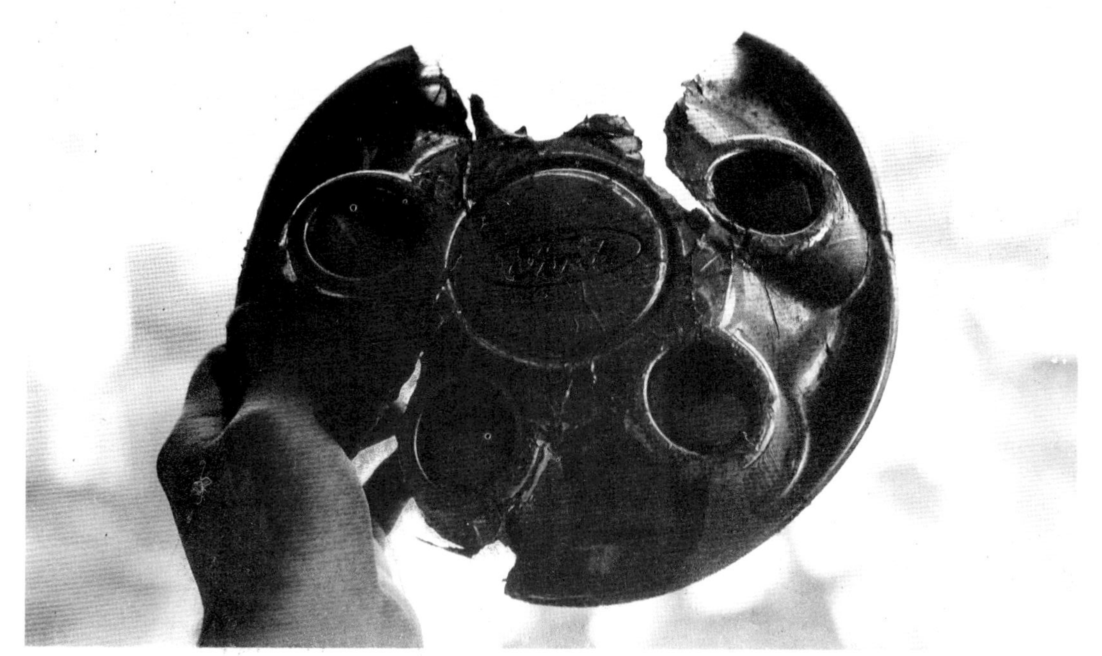